TABLE OF CONTENTS

Page

ACRONYMS

NSC   National Security Document

U.S.   United States

CHAPTER 1

INTRODUCTION

In modern times—with the rise of the national state, the expansion of European civilization throughout the world, the industrial revolution, and the steady advance of military technology—we have constantly been confronted with the interrelation of commercial, financial, and industrial strength on the one hand, and political and military strength on the other.[1]

— Edward Meade Earle

In 1992, Ethan Kapstein declared that "the International system is characterized by anarchy, by the absence of central authority. Within that anarchic world, states must pursue the twin goals of security and prosperity."[2] As today's national leaders pursue these twin goals, they must do so in a globalized world; one in which complete economic, political, and resource independence are no longer a reality. They must carefully administer the circular relationship between economic and informational strength (prosperity) on the one hand, and their ability to produce political and military strength (security) which in turn secures the former. Thus, in the current globalized environment, resources that enable national strength, act as a catalyst for conflict among states.

Our instruments of national power; diplomatic, information, military, and economic are inextricably linked with technology. In turn much of our most critical technology is dependent on continued access to strategic resources. Consequently, as new technology emerges, or existing technology advances, the strategic resources associated

---

[1]Peter Paret, *Makers of Modern Strategy: from Machiavelli to the Nuclear Age* (Princeton, NJ: Princeton University Press, 1986).

[2]Ethan B. Kapstein, *The Political Economy of National Security, a Global Perspective* (New York: McGraw-Hill, 1992), xiii.

with them may or may not change in value as well. These resources may decline in value, increase in value, or emerge as critically useful—such as rare earth materials have currently, in the computer industry.[3] The evolutionary interrelationship between technological advancement and the subsequent change in strategic resource value can be viewed as a transition period. During these periods of transition, nations may rapidly emerge into positions of great power or become extremely vulnerable due to a new found dependence. This may lead to resource conflict as nations continue their pursuit of prosperity and security. National leaders will inevitably change or adopt national security policies in congruence with their relative dependence, be it advantageous or not.

The purpose of this study is to examine technological strategic resource dependence, its potential for conflict in the twenty-first century, and subsequent influences on United States (U.S.) national security policy. The study will explore two major assumptions in particular. The first being whether or not nations were historically in a constant state of, or preparing for, armed conflict over strategic resources; specifically those linked to critical technologies that sustained economic prosperity and national security. The second is that the U.S. is currently in the early stages of a strategic resource transition period. If so, then mineral resources associated with computerization and advanced electronics will markedly increase in their strategic relative importance. This could result in increased competition and potential conflict with unexpected nations over the next 25 to 50 years, with subsequent challenges for U.S. national security policy.

---

[3]Eric Martin and Sonja Elmquist, "U.S. to File WTO Complaint Over China Rare-Earth Export Caps," 13 March 2012, http://www.bloomberg.com/news/2012-03-13/u-s-will-ask-for-wto-s-help-to-fight-chinese-curbs-on-rare-earth-exports.html (accessed 20 March 2012).

Given this, it would be prudent to examine historical examples for insights into what worked and what did not.

To gain insight, the study will explore five interrelated concepts within the context of three historical examples. The three historical examples will consist of the Age of Steam, the Age of Oil, and the Nuclear Age. The five interrelated concepts are the existence of macroinventions/microinventions, strategic resources and access, usage of instruments of national power specifically; military, effects on national security policy, and the concept of techno-resource-dependence transition periods. The intent is to garner insights into how U.S. national security policy may be influenced by the Information Age over the next 25 to 50 years. To do so, each of the historical examples will be examined separately. Several key terms and concepts that will be used throughout the study must be defined before advancing further.

The first two terms are "macroinvention" and "microinvention." They are borrowed from Joel Mokyr's book entitled *The Lever of Riches: Technological Creativity and Economic Progress*. The definitions are "inventions which embody a new idea, without clear precedence as to how they will ultimately affect society" and "small incremental steps that improve, adapt, and streamline existing techniques already in use, reducing costs, improving form and function, increasing durability, and reducing raw material requirements" respectively.[4] The third set of terms are instruments of national power; diplomatic (political), information, military, and economic. These are sources of power derived from national resources and means. The final term is techno-resource-

---

[4]Joel Mokyr, *The Lever of Riches: Technological creativity and Economic Progress* (New York: Oxford University Press, 1990).

dependence transition period. This is defined as the period between the emergence of a macroinvention and the point whereby a nation consciously assumes a level of dependence on this technology and its associated strategic resource to sustain and/or enhance an instrument of national power.

Four fundamental questions will shape the narrative for each of these chapters: what new strategic resource dependent technology emerged that had a direct impact on the nation's ability to wage war? What was the associated strategic resource(s) that allowed the production, sustainment, and operation of this new technology and what was the level of access? How did the nation employ its military instrument of national power to ensure access to the strategic resource(s)? And finally, what national security policy changes were made as a result of this new technology and the associated strategic resource? Considering these fundamental questions within the context of specific historical examples will hopefully provide valuable insights into which national security policies enhanced prosperity and security, and which did not.

When examining technological advancement, potential resource conflict, and the employment of national power in accordance with policy to ensure prosperity and security, the sheer number and magnitude of complex variables that come into play are staggering. These include: national energy consumption, availability and accessibility to natural resources, environmental concerns, national dependence and interdependence on raw materials, national industrial capacity, geopolitics, globalized economics, and privatized interest groups, to name only a few. Exploring the entirety of these variables within each of the historical examples is beyond the scope of this study. Therefore, the analysis in the subsequent chapters will focus primarily on those strategic resources and technologies that directly provided national military power. Furthermore, analysis

concerning changes in policy will focus primarily on those that had a direct link to the

ensured availability and accessibility of strategic resources, associated with building

national military power. Additional variables will be addressed only when it is absolutely

necessary to provide greater clarity or understanding.

The available literature for the topic of this research is divergent, largely

theoretical in nature, heavily weighted towards conflict over oil, and spread across

multiple books about political economics. That is, there is little to no literature that

directly addresses how technological advances may cause changes in the relative value of

strategic resources, other than as a subsection of macroeconomic issues. Additionally,

what literature is available tends to highlight the friction that resources cause between

privatized companies and their respective national governments, as opposed to the

friction between nation-states. Literature on resource dependence was primarily found in

economic sources and usually not tied to resource conflict. Whereas the literature on

resource conflict was found almost exclusively in political-economic sources and tended

to center on the oil industry specifically. Lastly, literature on national security policy was

found primarily in historical books and primary source documents.

Chapter 2 will center on Britain's experience during the Age of Steam. It

encompasses the years 1750 to 1900 and examines the period in history in which a series

of technological inventions and innovations harnessed steam as a source of power. The

Industrial Revolution in Britain accounts for the overwhelming majority of the historical

context. The steam engine is introduced as the dominant macroinvention of the period

and coal is considered the associated strategic resource. There are three major characteristics unique to Britain's example. First, as an island nation Britain's economic prosperity and security were largely dependent on its colonies and maritime power. Second, it had an abundance of coal within its national borders which allowed it to make full use of the technological advancements of the steam engine, most notably rapid industrialization. And third, Britain's rapid industrialization, thanks to an abundance of coal, had unintended consequences on its society, economy, and military.

Chapter 3 is comprised of Germany's experience in the Age of Oil from 1900 to the end of World War II. The historical context is divided into four specific historical periods: 1900 to the start of World War I, the First World War, the interwar period between the World Wars, and the Second World War. In this example the internal combustion engine is the dominant macroinvention and oil is the logical associated strategic resource. Germany's example highlights four unique characteristics pertaining to strategic resource dependence and conflict. The first is that Germany's leaders identified the techno-resource-dependence transition period early. This allowed them to institute successful economic reforms and specifically tailor their national security policies. The second is that Germany did not have adequate access to oil resources for Hitler's national aims. As such, Germany sought ways to increase access through alternative means. The third is that Germany employed its military in an attempt to capture additional oil resources. Finally, Germany failed to secure increased access to oil militarily.

Chapter 4 will discuss the U.S.' experiences in the Nuclear Age which, for the purposes of this study, begins post World War II and continues until one year after the fall of the Soviet Union. The historical context is set separated into three specific periods:

1939 to 1953 (the end of the Korean War), 1954 to 1962 (the Cuban Missile Crisis), and 1963 to 1992 (one year passed the fall of the Soviet Union). In this example nuclear fission is considered the macroinvention and uranium the associated strategic resource. The U.S.' example has three unique characteristics. The first, being that the purpose of the macroinvention and its associated resource were overwhelmingly related to national military power. The second is that the U.S. was initially concerned with "preventing" access to the strategic resource. However, once it was understood that uranium was relatively abundant, focus turned to preventing the proliferation of the macroinvention, nuclear fission. The final unique characteristic for the U.S.' example is that the relative abundance of uranium effectively negated the techno-resource-dependence transition period.

Chapter 5 is the last chapter of the study. It provides context for analysis by describing pertinent characteristics of the Information Age. It suggests that the Internet is the premiere macroinvention of the age and discusses the mineral resources associated with it. The primary purpose of chapter 5 is synthesizing insights gleaned from the previous three chapters, with the characteristics of the Information Age, to generate considerations for U.S. national security policy over the next 25 to 50 years. It concludes with final policy considerations and recommendations for future research.

CHAPTER 2

THE AGE OF STEAM

> A furnace had been lighted in Shropshire, fire from which was carried to a hundred new and larger furnaces, springing up not in silent woodland, but in busy haunts which the coalfields had already brought into being.[5]
>
> — T. S. Ashton

The first example will examine Britain's experience through the Industrial Revolution and the final decades of the nineteenth century. This period was chosen for five reasons. First, it adequately depicts all four aspects of the study's conceptual framework: the emergence of the steam engine as a strategic resource dependent macroinvention,[6] a techno-resource-dependent transition period,[7] how Britain acquired access to its coal supplies, and subsequent influence on national security policy. Second, Britain had unlimited access to coal within its national borders in relation to its goals. Third, Britain as an island nation was dependent on its colonial empire for economic survival. Fourth, Britain did not fully understand or accept the techno-resource-dependence transition period until much later in the example. Finally, this period serves as an excellent example because there is a wealth of literature and research surrounding the period.

---

[5]Thomas Southcliffe Ashton, *Iron and Steel in the Industrial Revolution* (Manchester, ND: Manchester University Press, 1924), 23.

[6]Inventions which embody a new idea, without clear precedence as to how they will ultimately affect society.

[7]The period between the emergence of a macroinvention and the point whereby a nation consciously assumes a level of dependence on this technology and its associated strategic resource to sustain and/ or enhance an instrument of national power.

The Age of Steam is difficult to define in exact years. It is roughly analogous to

the British Industrial Revolution, which many historians place between the years of 1750

to 1850.[8] More definitively, the Age of Steam refers to the period in history in which a

series of technological inventions and innovations harnessed steam as a source of power.

For the purposes of this study, the Age of Steam encompasses the years 1750 to 1900.

The latter part of the nineteenth century is included for two primary reasons. First, it fully

demonstrates Britain's ability to not only harness steam power, but in turn, translate it

into national economic and military power through industrialization and naval strength

respectively. Second, it provides a logical transition into the subsequent example, the Age

of Oil, as well as, facilitates a level of continuity between the two. The study now

addresses the four narrative questions within the context of the Age of Steam.[9]

To determine what strategic resource dependent macroinvention emerged in the

Age of Steam that had a direct impact on Britain's ability to wage war, this study will

need to briefly trace the origins of what is arguably the most important invention of the

Industrial Revolution, the steam engine. To do this, the study must temporarily expand its

scope prior to 1750, to explore the early theories and inventions which guided steam

power. Steam was first used as a power source in ancient Greece but was never put to any

---

[8]Charles More, *Understanding the Industrial Revolution* (New York: Routledge, 2000), 2.

[9]Narrative questions: What new strategic resource dependent technology emerged that had a direct impact on the nation's ability to wage war? What was the associated strategic resource that allowed the production, sustainment, and operation of this new technology and what was the level of access? How did the nation employ it military instrument of national power to ensure access to the strategic resource? What national security policy changes were made as a result of this new technology and the associated strategic resource?

serious use until much later. In the 1500s and 1600s steam was occasionally mentioned in scientific treatises, but it was not put to practical use until 1681, when the Frenchman Denis Papin invented the pressure cooker.[10] Ironically, it was here that the true story of steam power in Britain really began.

Denis Papin was born in Blois, France, in 1647. He became a student of medicine and, by the age of 22, was a physician. Shortly thereafter, he went to Paris to work with the famed scientist Christian Huygens who had learned about air pumps during a visit to the London laboratories of Robert Boyle in 1661.[11] The idea of air pumps and their ability to create motion greatly interested Papin. In 1673, while Papin was still working with Huygens in France, Huygens proposed an engine that he believed could be driven by gunpowder. However, by 1687, Papin soon saw that it would be impractical since it left so much "elastic" gas in the piston after each explosion.[12] Disheartened but not defeated, Papin later stumbled upon an answer to the elastic gas problem. He figured out that steam would condense to almost nothing and a piston stroke could be completed. Instead of exploding gunpowder to create pressure, he could condense steam to create a vacuum and let the exterior air pressure complete the working stroke. In 1690, Papin published the

---

[10]Andrea Sutcliffe, *Steam: The Untold Story of America's First Great Invention* (Gordonsville, VA: Palgrave Macmillan, 2004), 10.

[11]John H. Lienhard, *How Invention Begins: Echoes of Old Voices in the Rise of New Machines* (Oxford University Press, 2006), 51. Of note: Robert Boyle's experiments with pneumatics established the principle that the atmosphere was a fluid possessing weight and that its pressure could be excluded from the interior of a closed vessel so as to obtain a vacuum. This was later incorporated into the construction of the first steam engines.

[12]Ibid., 53.

design of a so-called atmospheric engine.[13] Papin used the atmospheric engine in a

variety of other inventions during the last decade of the seventeenth century. One in

particular, a pump which removed water from mines, caught the attention of English

inventors in 1695 and later helped spark the British industrial revolution.

Problems with access and persistent availability of energy resources for the iron

industry played a key role in the continued development of steam power. During the

sixteenth and early seventeenth century, the British iron smelting industry used firewood

and charcoal as the primary energy sources for operating its furnaces. K. K. Chatterjee, in

his book, *Uses of Energy, Minerals and Changing Techniques,* notes that "the

proliferation of iron furnaces in England and the consequent cutting of forests for

producing charcoal assumed such a magnitude that the British Parliament had to pass an

Act prohibiting further expansion of the industry. Then, in 1621 the iron-smelting

industry received an impetus when Dud Dudley discovered 'pit coal' as a viable

alternative to charcoal."[14] However, water accumulation in the pits hampered British coal

miner's extraction efforts, greatly reducing the efficiency of the mines. Horse drawn and

physical labor, which was slow and laborious, remained the only means of removing

water from the mines unless another method could be found.

Thomas Savery was born circa 1650 in Devonshire, England, on the country's

southwest coast. Little is known of his early life, but he probably worked in Devonshire's

tin or coal mines. He might also have served as an officer during military campaigns,

---

[13]Ibid.

[14]K. K. Chatterjee, *Uses of Energy, Minerals and Changing Techniques*
(Daryaganj, Delhi, India: New Age International, 2008), 16-17. Pit coal literally refers to
mineral coal dug from the earth which left large pits in the ground.

11

because he was well known to high-ranking political figures and was commonly called Captain Savery.[15] Savery became one of the most productive inventors of the seventeenth and early eighteenth centuries. Since he was from Devonshire, and most likely aware of the problems associated with water accumulation in the coal mines, Savery set out to capitalize on the work of Papin. In 1698 Savery introduced a device known as the "miner's friend" which was the first invention to harness steam power. It was meant to pump ground water from mines in England.[16] Unfortunately for Savery, his design, which required steam under pressure and was dangerous to operate as leaks and ruptures often occurred, ended up being a failure.[17]

As it turned out, Savery was not the only English inventor interested in the potential of steam power to increase the efficiency of the iron industry. Thomas Newcomen was born on 24 February 1663 in Dartmouth, England and is often acclaimed as the actual inventor of the steam engine.[18] Newcomen was an ironmonger by training, and he successfully converted Savery's primitive steam pump into a true, if inefficient, source of motive power.[19] Furthermore, Newcomen improved upon Savery's invention by introducing a cylinder and piston, which could be filled with steam pushing the piston

---

[15]Dennis Karwatka, "Thomas Savery and His Steam-Operated Water Pump," *Tech Directions* 66, no. 7 (2007): 100, http://search.proquest.com/docview/218494271?accountid=28992 (accessed 25 July 2012).

[16]Ibid.

[17]Neil Schlager and Josh Lauer, ed., "Thomas Newcomen," *Science and Its Times*, vol. 4 (Detroit: Gale, 2001), Gale Student Resources In Context, Web, 25 July 2012.

[18]Ibid.

[19]Noted by Neil Schlager and Josh Lauer.

one way and then cooled so that the steam condensed to form liquid water, leaving a near

vacuum so that air pressure would push the piston back.[20] Thus, the steam engine, which

facilitated numerous other microinventions, was born.[21] However, the "Newcomen

Engine" was not a total success. This was because "it was inefficient in that much of the

heat energy was wasted heating up the cylinder after each cooling."[22] This final setback

for the steam engine was overcome by the Scottish engineer James Watt, who eliminated

this problem by adding a separate condenser so that the cylinder could remain hot.[23] The

microinventions that emerged from the steam engine, which later had a direct impact on

Britain's national military power, were steam powered ships, railroad locomotives, and

machine powered factories.

With the macroinvention that emerged during the Age of Steam identified, the

study will now explore the second narrative question: what strategic resource was

associated with the steam engine and how available and accessible was it to Britain? As

noted, firewood and charcoal had been used for hundreds of years in Britain as a means

to provide energy for not only the iron industry, but local households as well. However,

for a variety of reasons, coal emerged as the dominant resource for providing steam

power not only in Britain, but many nations around the world. Among these reasons are:

availability, accessibility, quality, alternative sources, demand, and the ability to use it, to

---

[20]Ibid.

[21]Microinvention: small incremental steps that improve, adapt, and streamline
existing techniques already in use, reducing costs, improving form and function,
increasing durability, and reducing raw material requirements.

[22]Schlager and Lauer.

[23]Ibid.

name a few. Since the steam engine, through the use of coal and later coke, greatly increased the efficiency of factories, the demand for iron also increased throughout Britain during the Industrial Revolution. This created a greater need for an efficient means to transport these raw materials to its factories, which the locomotive and steamships later provided.

Britain enjoyed considerable availability and accessibility to coal and iron during the Industrial Revolution.[24] However, for coal specifically, the relative abundance and ease of access was not the primary reason for its emergence as the dominant strategic resource associated with the steam engine. E. A. Wrigley provides keen insights as to why coal became the dominant power source for the steam engine in Britain. Wrigley's reasoning for coal's rise to dominance centers around two key concepts: the "organic economy," which is generally defined as human sustenance and energy gained from cultivatable land and agriculture, and the "mineral-based energy economy," which is derived from expendable mineral resources.[25] Chris Evans, in his book, *The Industrial Revolution in Iron: The Impact of British Coal Technology in Nineteenth-Century Europe*, summarizes these concepts and their effect on nineteenth and twentieth century Britain well.

According to Evans, the British people understood that "since virtually everything necessary for the sustenance of human life—foodstuffs, raw materials and fuel—came

---

[24]Roy Church, *The History of the British Coal Industry, Volume 3 - 1830–1913: Victorian Pre-Eminence* (Oxford: Clarendon Press, 1986).

[25]Chris Evans, and Goran Ryden, *The Industrial Revolution in Iron: The Impact of British Coal Technology in Nineteenth-Century Europe* (Burlington, VT: Ashgate Publishing Company, 2005), 3-4.

from the land, the productivity of agriculture set limits to economic growth" and that "ultimately, the increased demand for food, for raw materials and energy would press too hard on the land." In short, Britain would have to convert to a mineral-based economy, which coal provided, if it wanted to keep up with the energy demands of the Industrial Revolution—which the steam engine had, in no small way, spawned. Therefore, coal necessarily became a major part of Britain's economy. Roy Church highlights this fact in his book, *The History of the British Coal Industry*, by stating that "it is difficult to exaggerate the importance of coal to the British economy between 1830 and 1913."[26] For better or worse, Britain had become, to a very high degree, dependent on coal as a means to power its industry.

The emergence of the steam engine and why coal became so important to Britain's continued prosperity during the Age of Steam have been, for the purposes of this study, satisfactorily explored. Given this, the study must now turn its attention to the third narrative question: how did Britain employ instruments of national power to ensure access and availability of this critical strategic resource? In short, it did not have to because it had abundance on the home isle. However, this came at the cost of other resources needed to continue Britain's growth and prosperity. Since the British feared their "organic economy" would reach capacity, and because their mineral-based economy had so rapidly increased the rate of industrial production, manufacturers sought access to resources and markets across the empire. That is, the British sought to sell goods in Asia and northern Europe and import textiles and foodstuffs from India and Africa. This would

_____

[26]Church, 758.

allow them to continue, and even increase, their use of coal to expand their industrial and economic strength.

Britain's position as a world power continued to rise. However, they would need to increase their, organic economy, through expansion and control of the empire. Therefore, in Britain's unique case, they employed their economic and military instruments of national power not so much to ensure access to coal, but to ensure continued and increased use of it. Specifically, the British Royal Navy ensured that their sea lanes and trade routes remained open and secure.[27] Robert K. Massie, in his book, *Dreadnought: Britain, Germany, and the Coming of the Great War*, notes that "more than half of the steamships plodding the oceans in 1897 flew the Red Ensign of the British merchant navy."[28] Additionally, the Army was employed as more of a Police Force to secure its ever-expanding empire. Without these, Britain would not have been able to import vital resources such as manganese, palm oil, and rubber to sustain production, nor could it trade the goods it manufactured to increase economic strength.

The study must now address the fourth and final narrative question: what national security policy changes were made as a result of this new technology and associated strategic resource? Since the term "national security policy" was not in use within the same context as it is today, specific treaties, political assertions, and military employment decisions will be explored to find answers to this question. Furthermore, it is not within the scope of this study to examine all of the national security policies and decisions that

---

[27]Robert K. Massie, *Dreadnought: Britain, Germany, and the Coming of the Great War* (New York: Random House, 1991), xxi.

[28]Ibid.

Britain may have made during the Age of Steam. Because the purpose is to explore how the rise of a specific technology and its associated strategic resource, in this case the steam engine and coal, ultimately affected policy, the study will focus on policy decisions made towards the end of the era. Therefore, in an attempt to glean insight from this era, the study will highlight specific treaties, security decisions, and the general security posture of the British Navy and Army during the final three decades of the nineteenth century.

During the final decades of the nineteenth century, Britain, like many of its rivals, was not only a colonial empire, but had adopted a policy of imperialism as well. Robert Johnson, in his book, *British Imperialism*, defines the British version of imperialism as "the exercise of power over the domains Britain controlled," but notes that "any definition must take account of the degree of influence it had beyond the imperial borders."[29] Although this definition is straightforward and highlights the importance of influence as an intangible, it does not shed light on the question of "why" Britain adopted this policy. On the other hand, Benjamin J. Cohen, in the book, *The Question of Imperialism: Political Economy of Dominance and Dependence*, provides a very insightful definition. According to Cohen: "It follows that if a state is to enhance its national security, it must, to the extent possible, try to use its foreign policy to reduce its dependence on others . . . it must try to enhance its net power position by increasing its own influence on others–that is to say, its dominance over them. This means that imperialistic behavior is a perfectly rational strategy of foreign policy. It is a wholly

---

[29]Robert Johnson, *British Imperialism* (Gordonsville, VA: Palgrave Macmillan, 2003), 1.

legitimate and logical response to the uncertainty surrounding the survival of the

nation."[30] Considering the concepts put forth by Wrigley of an, organic economy, and a

"mineral-based economy," along with the fact that Britain was an island based nation, it

becomes clear as to why a policy of imperialism, as described by Cohen, became an

attractive policy for the British. However, Britain was not the only nation to adopt this

policy in an attempt to expand its empire and influence, most of the European nations, as

well as Russia, and numerous Asian nations, were also.

It is important to note that Britain did not adopt a policy of imperialism

"overnight." Much to the contrary, the onset of steam power, and with it the industrial

revolution, were key factors in this incremental decision. Robert Johnson adequately

portrays this in the following: "By the 1800s, faced with the economic challenge of

industrialized competitors in Europe and America, and the military-naval challenge of

hostile powers, Britain redefined its imperial role. It sometimes appeared to be

consolidating and on the defensive, yet in the last 30 years of the nineteenth century, it

acquired 5 million square miles and 88 million new subjects. Strategically valued regions

became the focus of intense diplomatic interest or of military operations."[31] As expected,

the decision to adopt an imperialistic foreign policy, led to increased competition and

subsequent conflict with other nations.

By the mid 1880s almost the entire African continent had fallen to European

imperialism. With only a few territories remaining, notably Liberia and Ethiopia, the

---

[30]Benjamin J. Cohen, *The Question of Imperialism: Political Economy of Dominance and Dependence* (New York: Macmillan, 1974), 242-3.

[31]Johnson, 4.

potential for armed conflict between the imperialist nations loomed. Consequently, the

European powers decided to act diplomatically to preserve and exploit their gains.

Lawrence Sondhaus, in his book, *Naval Warfare, 1815-1914,* describes the first treaty,

known as the Berlin Conference of 1884 and 1885, enacted to deal with the situation. The

Berlin Conference of 1884 and 1885 regulated European colonization and trade in Africa

during the New Imperialism Period, and coincided with Germany's sudden emergence as

an imperial power. Called for by Portugal and organized by Otto von Bismarck, first

Chancellor of Germany, its outcome, the General Act of the Berlin Conference, can be

seen as the formalization of the Scramble for Africa.[32] Sondhaus goes on to note the

relative, if only temporary, success of the conference: "the conference ushered in a period

of heightened colonial activity by European powers, while simultaneously eliminating

most existing forms of African autonomy and self-governance." For the rest of the

nineteenth century, thanks to diplomacy backed by economic and military national

strength, Britain's organic economy remained secure.

Although the Berlin Conference of 1884 and 1885 assured Britain a level of

stability, especially on the African Continent in the short term, preparation for inevitable

conflict during this new era of imperialism continued. Subsequently, Britain began

formalizing its national security strategy by taking full advantage of its industrial and

military strength. Britain's Parliament instituted the Naval Defense Act of 1889 on 31

May 1889. The purpose of the act was to formally adopt the country's "two-power

standard" and increase Britain's naval strength, which called for the Royal Navy to

---

[32]Lawrence Sondhaus, *Naval Warfare, 1815-1914* (New York: Routledge, 2001),
161.

maintain a number of battleships at least equal to the combined strength of the next two largest navies in the world.[33] In 1889, France and Russia were considered the second and third largest navies in the world, followed closely by Germany. Therefore, national dominance, enabled by massive wealth and resources from colonies in Asia and Africa, required a first rate navy, which at the time, was protected by iron hulls and powered by steam engines.

British naval dominance did not come without a price. In the late nineteenth century the British Navy effectively provided the "collective security" of all trade being exported to or imported from the Indian subcontinent and other sea coasts of the world.[34] Michael W. Doyle, in his book *Empires*, explains that Britain was prepared to pay the costs because of the gain from trade, which would not have existed otherwise, offset the costs and because the navy was Britain's essential means of national security.[35] Steam power, enabled by coal, was critical to Britain's ability to provide, collective security. Richard Gorski, in *Maritime Labor: Contributions to the History of Work at Sea, 1500-2000*, emphasized this further by noting that "long distance oceanic operation only became an economic reality with the replacement of wooden hulls by iron . . . boilers capable of higher steam pressures . . . and the development of a network of coaling stations."[36]

---

[33]Ibid.

[34]Michael W. Doyle, *Empires* (Ithica, NY: Cornell University Press, 1986), 236.

[35]Ibid., 237.

[36]Richard Gorski, *Maritime Labor: Contributions to the History of Work at Sea, 1500-2000* (Amsterdam, Netherlands: Amsterdam University Press, 2008), 186.

As a maritime power, Britain's coaling stations were of critical strategic importance to their economic prosperity and security, especially those centered on their Cape route. In 1897 the British Admiralty reported: "It is impossible to over-estimate the strategic value of the Cape coaling station. In the probable event of the interruption in time of war of the Suez Canal route to the East, the Cape would at once become the most important coaling station of the Empire."[37] British coaling stations not only facilitated maritime operations, but also facilitated British penetration into the Indian and African interior via railroad. Consequently, British coaling stations had to be garrisoned for security. This exacerbated the policing requirements of the British Army. Keith Wilson, in his book *International Impact of the Boer War*, explains that the Cape route's defense had to protect the Royal Navy's main dockyard and repair facility at Simon's Town on the Cape peninsula, as well as other key British coaling stations in the region; St Helena, Cape Town, Durban, and Mauritius.[38] Thus, the importance of coaling stations was twofold. First, they increased economic efficiency and the ability to project military power. Second, they compounded Britain's dependence on coal, as she sought to maintain economic efficiency and police an ever-expanding empire.

During his presidential address to the British Association for the Advancement of Science in 1881, William Thompson, one of Britain's premiere scientists at the time, warned that Britain's energy base was precarious and that disaster was impending. Daniel Yergin explains that Thompson's fear was centered on the sustained availability of a

---

[37]Keith Wilson, *International Impact of the Boer War* (New York: Palgrave, 2001), 13.

[38]Ibid.

particular strategic resource—coal—which had generated the "Age of Steam" and fueled Britain's industrial strength throughout the nineteenth century, making it a world power.[39] Without this vital strategic resource Britain's industrial preeminence, and therefore its commercial and economic strength, would inevitably decline. This catastrophic decline would hinder its ability to project political and military strength to protect its resource rich colonies.

By the middle of the nineteenth century, Britain had been a world power for over 200 years, and the rise of steam power, at the onset of the Industrial Revolution certainly sustained that fact throughout the rest of the century. However, British policy makers were also aware that, without a stable mineral-based economy, their position as a world leader would be in danger. During the latter half of the eighteenth and first half of the nineteenth centuries, several technological innovations in the steam engine sparked a significant transition period, the Industrial Revolution.[40] Industrial automation, the railway locomotive, and steam powered ships were not only made possible by the steam engine, but enjoyed considerable innovations throughout the Industrial Revolution. Britain was among the first to capitalize on these new technologies, thus greatly increasing its industrial and economic strength, which in turn enhanced its political and military power for the protection of its colonies. Within 100 years, Britain would become the largest empire in history, spanning over 11 million square miles and controlling one-

---

[39]Daniel Yergin, *The Quest: Energy, Security, and the Remaking of the Modern World* (New York: The Penguin Press, 2011), 3.

[40]Thomas Crump, *A Brief History of the Age of Steam: From the First Engine to the Boats and Railways* (London: Avalon Publishing Group, 2007).

quarter of the world's population.[41] Consequently for Britain, the relative importance of coal as a means of industrial energy increased dramatically during the Industrial Revolution.

The steam engine allowed industrial factories to not only increase production of textiles, but advance the development of iron-making techniques as well. This facilitated the production of railways, locomotives, and iron hulled ships capable of storing and transporting greater quantities of good. Furthermore, this meant that Britain's Military, critical to the security and survival of an ever expanding colonial empire, could police its territories with greater efficiency. Perhaps most importantly, it allowed Britain to retain its naval superiority by building state of the art steam powered warships, such as the HMS Dreadnought, which ensured the security of the home isle.[42] At a time when post-Napoleonic armies numbered hundreds of thousands of troops, railway locomotives, unlike horse drawn wagons, made it possible to transport personnel and supplies efficiently over long distances. In effect, the introduction, and subsequent technological advancements of the steam engine, allowed Britain to quickly enter the industrial age and greatly increase its industrial and economic power. This in turn produced considerable political and military strength to protect its territories, albeit only as long as it ensured a stable mineral-based energy supply.

Britain's instruments of national power, specifically economic and military prowess, became inextricably linked with the technological advances of the industrial

---

[41]Lawrence James, *The Rise and Fall of the British Empire* (New York: St. Martin's Press, 1994), 353.

[42]Massie.

age; and thus industrial technology with strategic coal resources. As the steam engine advanced; making possible industrial automation, railway locomotives, and technologically superior steam powered ships, the relative strategic importance of Britain's coal reserves, along with the quantities needed to sustain Britain's new found industrial and military strength, increased substantially. The evolutionary interrelationship between the steam engine and the subsequent change in the importance of coal, as a means to supply its mineral-based energy needs, forced Britain into a distinct transition period. Consequently, Britain's position of power increased dramatically. However, to maintain this power Britain would need to greatly alter its security and economic policies on colonial policing, less it run the risk of becoming vulnerable due to a new found dependence on not only coal, but the need to supplement its organic economy through its colonies. Over the next 100 years, these changes in policy, specifically the adoption of an imperialistic foreign policy, would lead to resource conflict among other European powers, as Britain continued its pursuit of prosperity and security.

CHAPTER 3

THE AGE OF OIL

> If I had the Ural Mountains with their incalculable store of treasures in raw materials, Siberia with its vast forests, and the Ukraine with its tremendous wheat fields, Germany and the National Socialist leadership, would swim in plenty! [43]
>
> — Adolf Hitler

The second example will examine Germany's experience from 1900 to the end of World War II. Like the previous example, this period in Germany portrays all four aspects of the study's conceptual framework: the emergence of the internal combustion engine as the dominant strategic resource dependent macroinvention,[44] a techno-resource-dependent transition period,[45] the rise of oil as a strategic resource and Germany's attempts to increase and maintain access to it, and the subsequent influence on national security policy. Contrary to the first example, Germany's experience during this period is different in three ways. First, unlike Britain with coal, Germany did not have unlimited access to oil within the confines of its national borders in relation to its aims. Second, Germany was not an island nation dependent on its colonial empire for economic survival like Britain. Finally, Germany accepted the techno-resource-dependent

---

[43]Hitler's Labor-Front speech in Nuremberg, 12 September 1936.

[44]Inventions which embody a new idea, without clear precedence as to how they will ultimately affect society.

[45]The period between the emergence of a macroinvention and the point whereby a nation consciously assumes a level of dependence on this technology and its associated strategic resource to sustain and/ or enhance an instrument of national power.

transition period much earlier than Britain did with coal and aligned their national security policy accordingly.

For the purposes of this study, the Age of Oil refers to the period between 1900 and the end of World War II in 1945. This period was chosen for two primary reasons. First, it adequately highlights the rise of oil as a critical strategic resource and acknowledges the affects that the internal combustion engine had on societies throughout the world. Secondly, it sheds light on how the internal combustion engine and oil directly affected national security policy. It does not mean to imply that the internal combustion engine or oil were less important or ceased to affect national policy post World War II. It merely illuminates the affects that the internal combustion engine and oil had on national security policy through multiple microinventions.[46]

It is beyond the scope of this study to explain all of the linkages and consequences of the events that occurred in Germany during the Age of Oil. However, it is necessary to address major historical events to enhance understanding and provide context. To do so, the study will briefly describe these events during four specific periods: 1890 to the start of World War I, the First World War, the interwar period between the World Wars, and the Second World War. Once the historical context is addressed, the study will then turn to the four narrative questions[47] to guide the rest of chapter 3.

---

[46]Joel Mokyr's term for small incremental steps that improve, adapt, and streamline existing techniques already in use, reducing costs, improving form and function, increasing durability, and reducing raw material requirements. In this context, inventions which make use of the internal combustion engine in all forms. As they pertain to national military power—automobiles, tanks, planes, and warships.

[47]Four narrative questions: What new strategic resource dependent technology emerged that had a direct impact on the nation's ability to wage war? What was the associated strategic resource(s) that allowed the production, sustainment, and operation of

From 1890 to the start of World War I there are four major events that need to be highlighted to enhance understanding—two of which pre-date the period but their effects are greatly manifested within it. The first is the unification of Germany and establishment of the German Empire in 1871 when Otto Von Bismarck was chancellor. Ruth Henig notes in her book, *Origins of the First World War* that this "clearly altered the distribution of power within Europe and ushered in a new international order." The second event was the rapid industrialization of Germany from 1870 to 1914. The enormous expansion of the German economy after unification and the accompanying growth of German political ambition not only caused considerable alarm to the other European powers, but provided a purpose for colonial expansion in Africa.[48] The third major event, or rather series of events, was the establishment of alliances by all the European powers during this period. By the end of 1907, a Triple Entente between France, Britain, and Russia had come into being, facing a Triple Alliance of Germany, Austria-Hungary and Italy.[49] The fourth event, or trend in response to the ones listed above, was increased militarization by the European powers—most notably a naval "arms race" between Germany and Britain. Within the context of these four major events, the

---

this new technology and what was the level of access? How did the nation employ it military instrument of national power to ensure access to the strategic resource(s)? What national security policy changes were made as a result of this new technology and the associated strategic resource?

[48]Ruth B. Henig, *Origins of the First World War* (Florence, KY: Routledge, 1993), 2. Henig later explains that Germany's colonial expansion in Africa may have been more so to undermine the other European powers than for economic gain as was the case with Britain during the Age of Coal.

[49]Henig, 13.

assassination of Archduke Franz Ferdinand and his wife is considered by many historians, to be the spark that ignited World War I.

World War I, which occurred from 1914 to 1918, had three major events that are pertinent to the purpose of this study. The first of these was the emergence of the tank and the employment of the airplane—oil dependent microinventions of the internal combustion engine—which were intended to break the stalemate of trench warfare. The second was the signing of the Treaty of Versailles. According to the Treaty of Versailles, Germany had to accept guilt for the war under Article 231; adhere to strict military restrictions including the prohibition of tanks, armored cars, submarines, armed aircraft, and a 100,000 man army cap; pay war reparations in excess of $10.7 million; and was forced to give up land previously gained during the Franco-Prussian War of 1870 to 1871. The most detrimental of these was Article 231, the War Guilt Clause, because it "more than any other in the entire Treaty of Versailles, was to cause lasting resentment in Germany."[50] The third major event was the sheer cost of the war in both human and economic terms. In total, Germany and her allies lost over six million lives, both military and civilian. At the end of World War I Germany was in economic ruin due to massive debt, hyper inflation, high unemployment, and the immediate demand for reparations.[51] Such were the conditions in Germany as it entered the interwar period.

The interwar period in Germany was a time of both great suffering and innovation. There are four events that need to be highlighted from this period. The first was Germany's rearmament plan which began in the early 1920s, just three years after

---

[50]Ibid., 21.

[51]Ibid., 21-26.

the war and in direct contradiction to the Treaty of Versailles. This event in particular

demonstrates the early stages of the techno-resource-dependent transition period for

Germany and sets the stage for subsequent national security policy change. Harold

Winton, in his book, *Challenge of Change: Military Institutions & New Realities, 1918-*

1941, noted the following:

> It is a common belief that blitzkrieg—the concept of modern mechanized warfare
> with combined arms—was developed by the Nazis after Adolf Hitler became
> chancellor in 1933. Such a position stands in clear contradiction to the historical
> evidence. Except for the creation of armored and paratroop divisions in the 1930s,
> all of the primary doctrinal operational concepts that came to be known as
> blitzkrieg during World War II had been developed and were well in place as part
> of the mental equipment of the German army by the mid-1920s.[52]

The second was the rise and fall of Weimar Germany from 1919 to 1933. Many

historians view this period in three separate eras. The first era, deemed the "years of

turmoil," spanned 1919 to 1923 and was characterized by extreme political and economic

chaos. The second era, known as the Stresemann era; named after the chancellor of the

coalition government, Gustav Stresemann, who held nationalistic views and was against

the Treaty of Versailles, spanned 1924 to 1929. This era saw some political and economic

stabilization under Stresemann's nationalistic views. The third era, which spanned 1930

to 1933, essentially marks the collapse of Weimar Germany, due in large part to the Great

Depression of 1932.

The third major event that occurred during the interwar period is in direct

response to the collapse of the Weimar government; the insurgent rise of the Nazi party

---

[52]Harold R. Winton, *Challenge of Change: Military Institutions and New Realities, 1918-1941* (Lincoln, NE: University of Nebraska Press, 2000), 42. The author argues that the final phase of techno-resource-dependence comes later with the collapse of Weimar Germany and the rise of the Nazi Party.

throughout the 1920s and its capture of power on 30 January 1933 when Adolf Hitler was sworn in as chancellor. David Redles accurately portrays the circumstances in which Hitler's party came to power by noting that "the total chaos of the Weimar period, particularly in the early years, elicited a profound sense of collapse for many Germans, outwardly and inwardly. Perched on the edge of an abyss, the Nazis in particular came to believe that Germany, and indeed Aryan humanity in general, had reached a historic turning point."[53] Hitler's regime immediately instituted a course of change for not only Germany itself, but for all of Europe as well.

The fourth and final event that will be highlighted under the interwar period is the institution of the Four Year Plan in 1936 by the Nazi Party. The plan, originally intended to be complete by 1940, was essentially a series of economic reforms designed to improve Germany's deplorable economic condition, achieve a high degree of autarchy, especially in resources, and prepare the military for war.[54] It was largely in response to the Soviet Union's Five Year Plan, which, under Joseph Stalin's Communist Government, was intended to increase the Soviet Union's economic, industrial, and military power between the years of 1928 and 1932. Stalin's plan was near completion at the onset of the Four Year Plan. In effect, Hitler's Germany was in a race for war preparation with Stalin's Soviet Union.

---

[53]David Redles, *Hitler and the Apocalypse Complex: Salvation and the Spiritual Power of Nazism* (New York: New York University Press, 2005), 57.

[54]Hitler's Labor-Front speech in Nuremberg, 12 September 1936.

There are three salient points to be highlighted for World War II itself. The first is the scope of Hitler's ambitions because it alludes to what would be the corresponding resource requirements. David Redles captures Hitler's vision in the following:

> From the early 1920s, Hitler and his inner circle had conceived of the Nazi movement as one day creating a millennial Reich that was envisaged as a racially pure world empire led by the Nazis themselves. It was a world that could not be fully realized until a final battle against the demonic force of Jewish Bolshevism had been won, once and for all.[55]

The second point for World War II is that Hitler desperately sought to acquire additional oil resources from the Balkans and other regions. Daniel Yergin notes that "from the very start, the capture of Baku and the other Caucasian oil fields was central to Hitler's concept of his Russian campaign."[56] This relates directly to the first salient point because for Hitler the Russian campaign "was" his vision for creating a millennial Reich. Even though Germany had access to oil within its own borders, Hitler understood that it would not be enough to complete the Russian campaign. Consequently, the Germans planned Operation Blau in September 1942; an operation which was designed to secure key Caspian oil fields around Baku, that never occurred in light of stiff Soviet resistance. The German High Command displayed overconfidence by preemptively celebrating the capture of Baku, to include presenting a cake of the region to Hitler himself, before the operation even commenced.

The final point to address for World War II is the shortage of fuel for the German Army in late 1944 and early 1945. During the Battle of the Bulge, one of the primary

---

[55]Redles, 171.

[56]Daniel Yergin, *The Prize: The Epic Quest for Oil, Money, and Power* (New York: Simon and Schuster, 1991), 317.

factors that prevented Colonel Jochen Peiper's forces from continuing their drive to

Antwerp was the shortage of fuel. This was not the only reason for ultimate German

defeat, merely a key tactical example that demonstrated the key aspects of the study.

More importantly, this point illustrates that Hitler's understanding and basic assumption

that Germany would not have sufficient quantities and access to oil, within its own

borders to the Soviet Union, was in fact correct.

With historical context established, the study will now begin analysis of its key

concepts: the emergence of a strategic resource dependent macroinvention, the techno-

resource-dependence transition period, how Germany ensured availability and access to

the resource, and subsequent influence on national security policy. Like the previous

chapter, each of the four narrative questions will be used to guide the analysis.[57]

Germany's historical experience will be taken into direct account as each question is

examined.

What new strategic resource dependent technology emerged that had a direct

impact on the Germany's ability to wage war? For the Age of Oil, the technology that

emerged is unquestionably the most influential macroinvention of the twentieth century,

the internal combustion engine. Interestingly, the macroinvention that emerged as the

most influential during the Age of Oil has several commonalities with the one that arose

during the Age of Steam. In addition to both of them being engines, they both had

---

[57]Four narrative questions: What new strategic resource dependent technology
emerged that had a direct impact on the nation's ability to wage war? What was the
associated strategic resource(s) that allowed the production, sustainment, and operation of
this new technology and what was the level of access? How did the nation employ its
military instrument of national power to ensure access to the strategic resource(s)? What
national security policy changes were made as a result of this new technology and the
associated strategic resource?

profound impacts on societal interaction, industrialized production, and the rapid evolution of previous microinventions, specifically those related to warfare and movement.[58]

To fully understand Germany's remarkable ability to wage war during the 1940s this study will need to briefly trace the origins of the internal combustion engine. Vaclav Smil, in his book *Creating the Twentieth Century: Technical Innovations of 1867-1914 and Their Lasting Impact*, provided a concise history of the internal combustion engine. He separated the history into five stages, some being consecutive or partially overlapping, and others being concurrent.[59] Of note, Smil's third stage roughly coincided with the beginning of the Age of Oil as defined in this study.

The first stage embraces failed intermittent efforts to build explosively powered machines, a quest that goes back to the seventeenth century and whose pace picked up during the first half of the nineteenth century. The second stage encompasses the construction of commercially promising stationary machines, powered by coal gas during the 1850s and their subsequent improvements by Nicolas Otto and Eugene Langen. The third stage involves practical automotive designs that emerged with the development of a gasoline powered engine, first used in carriage like vehicles during the 1880s.[60] The

---

[58]Of note: both macroinventions greatly increased the frequency with which people from different cultures and societies came into contact. As a result, there was increased commercial, political, and economic competition.

[59]Vaclav Smil, *Creating the Twentieth Century: Technical Innovations of 1867-1914 and Their Lasting Impact* (Cary, NC: Oxford University Press, 2005), 100.

[60]This coincides with the enormous expansion of the German economy after unification under Otto Von Bismarck and the accompanying growth of German political ambition.

fourth stage, which also includes pioneering reciprocating engines for the first airplanes, entails the rapid maturation of high performance four-stroke engines and the gradual emergence of road vehicles. The fifth and final stage, largely concurrent with the fourth, was marked by the first steps toward highly efficient mass production of automotive engines and other car parts.[61]

The study will now direct its focus to the microinventions that arose from the internal combustion engine, specifically those that had a direct impact on Germany's ability to wage war. The most pertinent microinventions being the automobile (armored car and truck), tank, airplane (fighter and bomber), and gasoline powered naval vessels (battleships, carriers, submarines, and logistical ships). While there were numerous microinventions that contributed to Germany's industrial and economic power which in turn provided military strength, it remains beyond the scope of this study to examine the entirety of these relationships. Therefore, only those relating directly to national military power will be explored further. Lastly, since the Age of Oil in Germany was divided into four distinct periods,[62] each microinvention will be discussed in relation to the period that it emerged.

At a time when Germany had upset the balance of power by establishing its Empire, had formed the Triple Alliance, was in a naval arms race with Britain, and the economy was thriving in light of rapid industrialization, several microinventions emerged: the automobile, airplane, gasoline powered battleship, aircraft carrier, and

---

[61]Smil, 101-102.

[62]Four specific periods: 1890 to the start of World War I, the First World War, the interwar period between the World Wars, and the Second World War.

submarine.[63] For the purposes of this study, the use of the term "emerged" is implies invented and successfully tested. This distinction is important because although almost all of the pertinent microinventions had emerged prior to or during World War I, Germany did not employ many of them until World War II. Interestingly, Germany only built one aircraft carrier, the *Graf Zeppelin*, which was never fully completed and therefore did not see action.

By mounting an internal combustion engine on a three-wheel chassis in 1886, German innovator Karl Benz, credited as the inventor of the automobile, unknowingly established the underpinnings of motorized warfare.[64] During World War I and II, trucks and armored cars, such as the Bussing A5P and Leichter Panzerspahwagen respectively, became integral to such military operations as reconnaissance, troop movement, and logistical resupply. The airplane emerged during this period as well. Originally invented in 1903 by the Wright Brothers, "the airplane evolved from a new, relatively primitive weapon into a powerful combat-effective weapon by the end of world War I."[65] The last microinvention to address during this period was so successful that many nations sought to ban it entirely post World War I. Harold Winton notes that "the submarine became one

---

[63]Note: while petrol powered battleships were beginning to emerge, specifically in Britain and the United States, Germany did not use all-oil firing for surface warships until after World War I. See Erik J. Dahl, "Naval Innovation: From Coal to Oil," *Joint Forces Quarterly* (Winter 2000-2001): 55.

[64]Smil, 99-100.

[65]Winton, 36.

of the primary weapons of naval warfare and was used as a strategic, almost war winning, weapon."[66]

World War I, which encompasses the second historical period, is characterized by the seemingly unbreakable stalemate of trench warfare. The horrific continuous loss of human life and mounting economic ruin, synonymous with this form of war, eventually led the Allies, forcing Germany to the Treaty of Versailles. Both the Central Powers and the Triple Entente desperately sought ways to break the stalemate. One of the answers to this problem was an ominous microinvention: the tank. The tank was developed during the course of the war and by 1918 thousands of tanks were serving on the front lines.[67] Although the airplane emerged in the previous period, it came of age as a weapon of war during World War I. By 1918, fast all metal aircraft, were not only supporting ground operations but conducting strategic air bombardment deep into the enemy homeland.[68]

The interwar period did not witness the emergence of any new microinventions per se. Instead, it became a period of intense innovation and rapid evolution of the ones that emerged in the previous period. This is remarkable for Germany, in light of the intense restrictions emplaced by the Treaty of Versailles and the economic turmoil that accompanied the rise and fall of Weimar Germany. Germany's rearmament during the early 1920s laid the groundwork for many of these technological advances, and the Four Year Plan provided the political and economic means to enact them. For most of the interwar period, Hitler's military strength and modernization lagged behind that of its

---

[66]Ibid.

[67]Ibid.

[68]Ibid., 36-37.

potential adversaries. Murray notes that the Soviets had established their first mechanized corps in the fall of 1932, three years before the first German Panzer divisions.[69] However, by the outbreak of World War II Germany had built one of the best, if not the best, military force in the world.

Like the interwar period, World War II did not see the emergence of any new microinventions derived from the internal combustion engine. Nevertheless, innovation and technological advancement continued. An excellent example of technological advancement during this period is the Messerschmitt Me 262, the first operational jet fighter. Although the Me 262 was not mass produced until late 1944 and was therefore unable to affect the course of the war, it did mark a critical turning point for combat aviation. Germany's military experience in World War II, characterized by mechanized maneuver supported by integrated air support, demonstrated a fundamental fact of modern warfare, techno-resource-dependence, was complete.

Critical to the understanding of how the key concepts of this study relate to the Age of Oil, it is important to note that the development of the internal combustion engine was nearly complete by the outbreak of WWI (the one exception being the advent of the jet engine). Smil exhibits this fact well: "remarkably, nearly all of the basic challenges of durable design and affordable car (combustion engine) manufacturing were resolved in a highly effective fashion before WWI."[70] Smil's note is important because it demonstrates two important and interrelated facts. The first is that derivative microinventions of the

---

[69]Williamson Murray and Allen R. Millett, *A War to Be Won: Fighting the Second World War, 1937-1945* (Cambridge, MA: Harvard University Press, 2001), 25.

[70]Smil, 102.

internal combustion engine were in use and understood. The second is that the need for

oil, and therefore continued access to it was inherent. Finally, noting that stage three and

four of Smil's developmental stages for the internal combustion engine roughly

correspond with the first two historical periods set forth in the Age of Oil, sheds light on

the concept of a resource-dependence transition period.[71] This will become more

apparent as the study transitions to the second narrative question.

What was the associated strategic resource(s) that allowed the production,

sustainment, and operation of the internal combustion engine and its derivative

microinventions, and what was Germany's level of access? There are numerous strategic

resources associated with the internal combustion engine and the microinventions[72] that

flowed from it. Among these are, iron ore, coal (used in factory operation), barium and

magnesium (used to manufacture rubber), petroleum, and aluminum. This study will

specifically focus on petroleum for two reasons. First, Germany's example uniquely

identifies conflict over its access, availability, and dependence which directly influenced

national security policy. Second, for many nations oil became the dominant strategic

resource of the twentieth century.

---

[71]According to Vaclav Smil, the third stage involves practical automotive designs that emerged with the development of a gasoline-powered engine first used in carriage-like vehicles during the 1880s. The fourth stage, which also includes pioneering reciprocating engines for the first airplanes, entails the rapid maturation of high-performance four-stroke engines and the gradual emergence of road vehicles. The first historical period is from 1890 to the start of World War I and the second comprised the First World War.

[72]For the purposes of chapter 3, the microinventions that derived from the internal combustion engine are automobiles, airplanes, tanks, and all petrol powered naval vessels.

Continued access to oil became synonymous with security and prosperity. As such, nations that controlled oil rich territories enjoyed significant political and economic power, and therefore, the potential for military power to ensure the former two. The Soviet Union had access to three times more oil than Germany did prior to the start of Operation Barbarossa, Germany's invasion of the Soviet Union, in June of 1941. Most of the Soviet Union's oil production came from the Caspian oil fields, specifically those around the city of Baku. This gave the Soviet Union a considerable advantage over the Germans.

Although oil products were in use during the nineteenth century, the strategic value of oil as a national security concern did not arise until after the invention of the internal combustion engine. Daniel Yergin, in his book, *The Prize: the Epic Quest for Oil, Money, and Power*, makes the following observation: "at the end of the 19th century, John D. Rockefeller had become the richest man in the United States, mostly from the sale of kerosene. Gasoline was then only an almost useless byproduct, which sometimes . . . was run out into rivers at night."[73] However, by the onset of World War I, national leaders had begun to understand the rise of oil's strategic value. Winston Churchill understood the risks of converting the Royal Navy to an all oil fleet vice coal, in 1911 when he stated, "in a word, mastery itself was the prize of the venture."[74] Understanding and accepting oil's strategic value was only part of the equation; the other was acquiring uninterrupted and efficient access to it. Winston Churchill described the difficulties of

---

[73]Yergin, *The Prize*, xvi.

[74]Winston S. Churchill, *The World Crisis,* vol. 1 (New York: Scribner's, 1923), 133.

acquiring uninterrupted access prior to the World War I by noting that "the oil supplies of the world were in the hands of vast oil trusts under foreign control."[75]

As previously noted, all of the primary doctrinal operational concepts that came to be known as blitzkrieg during World War II had been developed and were well in place by the mid 1920s. However, one problem still needed to be solved before the concepts could be fully implemented, finding and securing access to oil. As a highly developed industrial state, Germany was dependent, even in the peacetime of the 1930s on external sources for an adequate supply of oil.[76] Solving this very problem became a top priority of Hitler's even prior to his rise to power in January 1933. In a meeting with two IG Farben (a large German chemical company) officials in June 1932, Hitler discussed one possibility of achieving autarky through the manufacturing of synthetic fuels. Lecturing and declaiming his plans to motorize Germany and build new highways, Hitler declared that "today, an economy without oil is inconceivable in a Germany which wishes to remain politically independent. Therefore, German motor fuel must become a reality, even if this entails sacrifices."[77]

Under the four year plan, Hitler's synthetic fuel program did achieve a high level of success prior to the outbreak of World War II. However, Germany was still dependent on foreign supplies of oil. In 1938, German oil supplies came from three different

---

[75]Ibid.

[76]Peter J. Becker, "The Role of Synthetic Fuel In World War II Germany: Implications for today?" *Air University Review* (July-August 1981), http://www.airpower.maxwell.af.mil/airchronicles/aureview/1981/jul-aug/becker.htm (accessed 19 September 2012), 2.

[77]Yergin, *The Prize*, 312.

sources: imports of crude and finished petroleum products from abroad, production by

domestic oil fields, and syntheses of petroleum products from coal.[78] Dr. Peter Becker

provides a very revealing breakdown of Germany's access to oil:

> In 1938, of the total consumption of 44 million barrels, imports from overseas
> accounted for 28 million barrels or roughly 60 percent of the total supply. An
> additional 3.8 million barrels were imported overland from European sources (2.8
> million barrels came from Romania alone), and another 3.8 million barrels were
> derived from domestic oil production. The remainders of the total, 9 million
> barrels were produced synthetically.[79]

Before turning to the third narrative question, the study will consider Germany's

access and availability to other strategic resources in relation to oil to provide clarity.

Although World War I had decimated Germany's economy, the infrastructure developed

during rapid industrialization prior to the war remained, for the most part, intact along

with access to resources. Ruth Henig offers the following: "By 1910, Germany produced

three times as much iron as France, four times as much steel, and seven times as much

coal. In steel production, German furnaces turned out two-thirds of the European total—a

greater quantity than Germany's main rivals, Britain, France and Russia, put together."[80]

Oil remained Hitler's primary strategic resource problem.

The study now turns to the third narrative question: how did Germany employ its

military instrument of national power to ensure access to oil? As history has shown,

incrementally at first; and later, failed attempts to capture the Caucasus regions all at

once. More specifically, Hitler used his military as an occupation force, as a source of

---

[78]Becker, 1.

[79]Ibid.

[80]Henig, 8-9.

intimidation to secure political cooperation, and finally, for all out invasion. Although

beyond the scope of this study, it is important to note that prior to the start of World War

II Hitler quite skillfully incorporated diplomacy into his overall vision for expansion of

the Third Reich. Diplomatic examples include the Anti-Comintern Pact (anti-communism

pact) with Japan in 1936, the Pact of Steel (Rome-Berlin pact) with Italy in 1939, and the

Molotov-Ribbentrop Pact (non-aggression pact) with the Soviet Union in August of 1939.

Employing the German military incrementally, Hitler first ordered the occupation

of the Rhineland in 1936 to test the response of France and Britain. Acknowledging the

grave risk of this move, Hitler later remarked that those 48 hours were the most "nerve-

racking in my life."[81] Embolden by his success in the Rhineland, Hitler ordered the

occupation and subsequent annexation of Austria in March of 1938. Before the

annexation of Austria in 1938, oil fields in Germany were concentrated in northwestern

Germany. After 1938, the Austrian oil fields were also available, and the expansion of

crude oil output was chiefly affected there. Primarily as a result of this expansion,

Germany's domestic output of crude oil increased from approximately 3.8 million barrels

in 1938 to almost 12 million barrels in 1944.[82] By incrementally employing its military

instrument of national power, Germany had in fact improved its access to oil. At the

outbreak of the war, Germany's stockpiles of fuel consisted of a total of 15 million

barrels. The campaigns in Norway, Holland, Belgium, and France added another 5

million barrels in booty.[83]

---

[81]Yergin, *The Prize*, 316.

[82]Becker, 2.

[83]Ibid.

By late 1938, the mere threat of Germany's army began to illicit political and economic cooperation from neighboring states. Even before the Russian prospects had come to naught, Romania, specifically the Ploesti oil fields, had developed into Germany's chief overland supplier of oil. Under internal pressure to choose sides or risk invasion, Romania officially joined the Axis Powers in November 1940. As a result, Romania's exports to Germany increased from 2.8 million barrels in 1938, to 13 million barrels by 1941, a level that was essentially maintained through 1942 and 1943. This amounted to almost half of Romania's total production.[84] The oil imported from the Ploesti oil fields in Romania were the most significant source of oil for Germany throughout the war, second only to their synthetic fuel plants established under the Four Year Plan.

Although the annexation of Austria and alliance with Romania increased Germany's access to oil somewhat, Hitler knew that this would not be enough to accomplish his overall goal of achieving victory in a "final battle against the demonic force of Jewish Bolshevism." In June 1941, Hitler decided that it was time to employ the German Army all against the Soviet Union, a direct violation of the Molotov-Ribbentrop Pact. In a secret telegram to the German Ambassador to the Soviet Union, Hitler wrote: "the Führer has therefore ordered the German military to oppose this threat with all the means at their disposal."[85] Albert Speer, the German Minister for Armaments and War

---

[84]Ibid.

[85]German Declaration of War on the Soviet Union, 21 June 1941. Paragraph VI, sub point 3.

Production, said at his interrogation in May 1945, "the need for oil was certainly a prime motive" in the decision to invade the Soviet Union.[86]

Securing additional oil resources became a matter of survival for Hitler's Third Reich. If the oil of the Caucasus, along with the "black earth" (the farmlands of the Ukraine), could be brought into the German empire, then Hitler's New Order would have within its borders the resources to make it invulnerable.[87] Peter Becker notes that "the smallest of the Russian oil fields at Maikop was captured in August 1942, and it was expected that the two remaining fields and in Grozny and Baku also would fall into German hands. Had the German forces been able to capture these fields and hold them, Germany's petroleum worries would have been over."[88] Fortunately, this never came to pass; German ground forces began to run out of fuel as early as December 1944.

The study now turns to the fourth and final narrative question: what national security policy changes were made as a result of this new technology and the associated strategic resource? Germany most certainly did not want to relive the horrific experiences of World War I associated with trench warfare. As such, the concepts of mobile warfare were fresh in the minds of Germany's military leaders throughout the 1920s. What they required were the practical means to employ these concepts. The microinventions of the internal combustion engine; tanks, planes, armored cars, and motorized transport would provide just that. However, Germany needed a strong national security policy to achieve this goal.

---

[86]Yergin, *The Prize*, 317.

[87]Ibid.

[88]Becker, 2.

There were three overarching national security policy changes made as a result of this new technology and the associated strategic resource oil. The first was to completely modernize the lead combat formations (armored divisions) of the German Military by making them a predominantly motorized force. This entailed key doctrinal and organizational changes within the German Military. The formation of panzer divisions and reorganization of the Luftwaffe to support ground operations are key examples. This required additional resources, primarily greater access to oil, and infrastructure development; primarily highway improvement and refinery construction.

The second set of national security policies were primarily addressed through the Four Year Plan. Of major concern was the inadequate access to oil. In 1934, German crude oil production was 300,000 tons annually and a number of measures were taken to step up the rate of exploration drilling. To increase efficiency, a law was passed nationalizing the ownership of oil, allowing the government to allocate exploration and exploitation rights in separate areas to individual companies.[89] Daniel Yergin notes that "by 1937-38, (IG Farben) was no longer an independent company, but rather an industrial arm of the German state, and fully Nazi-fied."[90] This policy facilitated the rapid construction and expansion of the Nazi war machine in preparation for war.

The third policy involved using the German armed forces as the primary means by which to expand the empire. The ability to rapidly advance into foreign territory and occupy it before an opponent could adequately respond greatly influenced Hitler's

---

[89]Official Report on German e-crude oil production during World War II, http://www.fischer-tropsch.org/primary_documents/gvt_reports/MofFP/ger_syn_ind/ (accessed 10 September 2012).

[90]Yergin, *The Prize*, 316.

decisions from 1939 to 1940. The concept of "blitzkrieg" became central to the employment of the German Military. So ingrained was this concept, that during the early hours of Operation Barbarossa, Hitler boasted that "we'll kick the door in and the house will fall down."[91] It was a policy that, arguably, proved to be Germany's undoing as it lost access to the one vital resource it needed, oil.

What conclusions can be drawn from Germany's example? Germany's example, in contrast to Britain's in the previous chapter, provides four unique insights. The first pertains to the early identification of the techno-resource transition period. Germany identified in the 1920s that they were transitioning to an age of mobile warfare and would therefore become dependent on oil. This allowed them to do two critical things. First, it allowed them to enact national security policies during the 1930s that would increase access to the vital strategic resource associated with the microinventions that emerged. Second, by understanding that they were not only becoming dependent, but that this dependence would increase, Germany was able to calculate its relative need versus its relative access and availability. In doing so, they identified the need to increase access and availability through other means, specifically through synthetic fuel. This in turn helped them overcome the relative shortage of oil reserves within their own borders, and ensured they were not entirely dependent on just one type and source. Combined, these two insights allowed them to produce tanks, planes, trucks, and armored cars while simultaneously increasing their access to oil.

The second conclusion is that Germany identified and understood the potential of the new technology as it pertained to the problem of mobile warfare. That is, they did not

---

[91]Ibid., 318.

just accept the new technology and then apply it to the former principles of "static warfare." One could argue that France did not perceive the potential of these new microinventions in quite the same way as Germany. However, that remains a topic for another discussion. Either way, the fact that the German Military adopted and employed these new technologies at the onset of World War II, is germane to this study.

The third conclusion is closely related to the second. Germany's rearmament program, in light of these new technologies and strategic resource dependency, was specifically tailored to their security environment. Post World War I Germany understood its position as a European Continent Nation; one whose primary security threats lie to the immediate west and east. Given this, German's national security policy applied its resources primarily to the buildup of the ground and air forces vice their navy.[92] This does not mean to imply that they did not invest time, resources, and effort into their navy. It merely seeks to illuminate the fact that German logisticians, engineers, and policy makers demonstrated forethought in tailoring their national security policy in accordance with the microinventions that emerged, the availability and access to oil, and their specific security situation.

The final conclusion centers on Germany's failure to secure critical oil resources in the Caucasus region. Germany identified the techno-resource transition period early, which allowed them to correctly determine that they would need to secure greater access to oil resources, to achieve their overall goal of defeating the Soviet Union. Therefore, the oil fields surrounding Baku were deemed critical to overall success. This led to the

---

[92]Germany invested significant resources in surface warfare ships and submarines. However, Germany only built one aircraft carrier prior to World War II which was never fully completed and never saw operation.

planning of Operation Blau which ended in failure. Although there are numerous reasons why Germany ultimately failed to secure critical oil resources in the Caucasus region, two in particular stand out. First, Germany neglected to motorize its support units. In 1941, only 25 percent of their ground forces were motorized; the overwhelming majority being combat vehicles specifically. Consequently, their supply lines could not keep up with combat formations. Second, Hitler's overconfidence in blitzkrieg tactics led him to prioritize northern sectors of the Soviet front over the seizure of Baku, even though he understood the extreme importance of the oil fields.

CHAPTER 4

THE NUCLEAR AGE

> This little bottle contains about a pint of uranium oxide; that is to say about fourteen ounces of the element uranium . . . and in this bottle, ladies and gentlemen, in the atoms . . . there slumbers at least as much energy as we could get by burning a hundred and sixty tons of coal.[93]
>
> — Professor Rufus

The study now turns to the third and final example: the U.S. from 1945 to 1992. Just like the previous two periods, the Nuclear Age also captures all four aspects of the studies conceptual framework.[94] However, the characteristics of the macroinvention and its associated strategic resource in the Nuclear Age differ from the previous chapters substantially. In the Nuclear Age, the macroinvention "nuclear fission" is just as much a process as it is a technological invention. The strategic resource, in this case uranium, is extremely unique in this example because the U.S. finds that it has more than it may ever need, for its military purposes towards the end of the period. Interestingly, the unique phenomenon attached to the macroinvention and strategic resource in this example effectively negate the techno-resource-dependent transition period to a large extent.[95]

---

[93]H. G. Wells, *The World Set Free* (London: Macmillan and Company, 1914), 24.

[94]The emergence of a strategic resource dependent *macroinvention*, a techno-resource-dependent transition period, the rise of uranium as a strategic resource, the United States' attempts to increase and maintain access to it, and subsequent influence on national security policy.

[95]The period between the emergence of a macroinvention and the point whereby a nation consciously assumes a level of dependence on this technology and its associated resource to sustain and/ or enhance an instrument of national power.

Because of this, the national security policy becomes dependent on "preventing" access to the strategic resource and the process by which it can be used—nuclear fission.

For this study, the Nuclear Age refers to the period between 1945 and 1992. It was chosen as an example for three reasons. First, because of the overwhelming impact the microinventions,[96] specifically nuclear weapons, had on the U.S.' ability to wage war. Second, the phenomena attached to the macroinvention and strategic resource described above is indeed uniquely different from previous periods. Third, the end of this period leads directly into the Information Age, which is a focal point for the overall purpose of this study.

As with previous periods, this study does not mean to suggest that nuclear fission, the macroinventions derived from nuclear fission, or uranium as a strategic resource have ceased to influence national security policy post 1992. Indeed, even a cursory look at the current national security policies of the U.S. demonstrates the contrary. More precisely, the years 1945 and 1992 serve as convenient "bookends" for the rise and decline of the threat of global nuclear war. Finally, it will be necessary to temporarily predate the period to address the rise of nuclear power.

Although the Cold War between the U.S. and the former Soviet Union is not the focus of this chapter, the study acknowledges the profound influence that it had on many of the aspects that will be examined. Therefore, it must be made clear that this study does

---

[96]Joel Mokyr's term for small incremental steps that improve, adapt, and streamline existing techniques already in use, reducing costs, improving form and function, increasing durability, and reducing raw material requirements. In this context, inventions which make use of nuclear fission in all forms. As they pertain to national military power—nuclear weapons, nuclear powered aircraft carriers, nuclear powered submarines, and nuclear reactors as a means to accomplish fission.

not intend to explain causes and effects of the Cold War specifically. Instead, the Cold War will provide an overwhelming amount of the historical context through which the study's concepts will be explored. The historical context for this chapter will be divided into three specific periods: 1939 to 1953 (the end of the Korean War), 1954 to 1962 (the Cuban Missile Crisis), and 1963 to 1992 (one year passed the fall of the Soviet Union). As with the two previous chapters, once the historical context is established the remainder of chapter 4 will be guided by the four narrative questions.[97]

The first historical period has three major events that need to be discussed to enhance understanding of the Nuclear Age. The foremost major event that occurred during the first historical period is the Manhattan Project. In the summer months of 1939 the work of scientists Joliot, Fermi, and Szilard in America had increased the possibility of starting a nuclear chain reaction in a large mass of uranium, and in doing so; generate vast amounts of power and large quantities of new radium-like elements.[98] News of this new possibility spread rapidly throughout the scientific community and on 2 August 1939, renowned physicist Albert Einstein informed President Roosevelt through a letter that:

> Now it appears this could be achieved in the immediate future. This phenomenon would also lead to the construction of bombs, and it is conceivable, though much less certain—that extremely powerful bombs of a new type may thus be

[97]The four questions that specifically guide each example through the conceptual framework: What new resource dependent technology emerged that had a direct impact on the nation's ability to wage war? What was the associated resource(s) that allowed the production, sustainment, and operation of this new technology and what was the level of access? How did the nation employ it military instrument of national power to ensure access to the resource(s)? What national security policy changes were made as a result of this new technology and the associated resource?

[98]Howard J. Langer, *World War II* (Westport, CT: Greenwood Press, 1999), 247.

constructed. A single bomb of this type, carried by boat and exploded in a port, might well destroy the whole port, together with some of the surrounding territory.[99]

With war looming in Europe, the research and development program intended to produce the atomic bomb began modestly in the fall of 1939. The combined program between the U.S., Britain, and Canada would later come to be known as the "Manhattan Project." American physicist Robert Oppenheimer and Major General Richard Groves headed the Manhattan Project's science and military operational groups. Together, they supervised thousands of scientists during World War II at Los Alamos, New Mexico.[100] Interestingly, within two years of the start of the Manhattan Project, the U.S. would find itself involved in the second major event of this period, World War II.

World War II is undoubtedly one of the most influential events of the twentieth century. Howard Langer, in his book *World War II*, notes the following influence it had on the U.S.: "there was no period like it in all of American history. The years from Pearl Harbor to V-J Day were a time of the greatest American unity ever."[101] However, in May 1940, a full year and a half prior to the U.S.' official entry into the war, the American people were not completely united. President Roosevelt, understanding the seriousness of the situation in Europe, addressed Congress on 16 May 1940 with the following message:

> These are ominous days—days whose swift and shocking developments force
> every neutral nation to look to its defenses in the light of new factors. The brutal
> force of modern offensive war has been loosed in all its horror. New powers of

---

[99]Ibid.

[100]Ibid.

[101]Ibid., xiii.

destruction, incredibly swift and ready, have been developed; and those who wield them are ruthless and daring.[102]

President Roosevelt would later turn to the American people for support. On the evening of 29 December 1940, Franklin Delano Roosevelt made one of the most important speeches of his presidency. Customarily for him at the time, he conducted his "Fireside Chats" via radio as a means to communicate and explain his policies to the American people. This time, he began: "This is not a fireside chat on war. It is a talk on national security, because the nub of the whole purpose of your President is to keep you now, and your children later, and your grandchildren much later, out of a last-ditch war for the preservation of American independence and all of the things that American independence means to you and to me and to ours."[103] Attempting to impress upon the American people the severity of the situation, he went on to add that the Nazi "masters of Germany have made it clear that they intend not only to dominate all life and thought in their own country, but also to enslave the whole of Europe, and then use the resources of Europe to dominate the rest of the world."[104] America officially entered the war after the attack on Pearl Harbor by the Japanese on 7 December 1941, somewhat ironically not in response to the threat of Nazi Germany.

---

[102]Ibid., 27. President Roosevelt's address to Congress, calling for an increase in defense spending, May 16, 1940. Of note: President Roosevelt's mention of "new powers of destruction, incredibly swift and ready, have been developed" is not necessarily speaking about atomic weapons. Although, by May of 1940 some scientists were beginning to ponder the possibility of a German atomic weapon program.

[103]Julian E. Zelizer, *Arsenal of Democracy: The Politics of National Security - From World War II to the War on Terrorism* (New York: Basic Books, 2009), 1.

[104]Ibid.

America and her allies were officially at war with the Axis Powers and the Empire of Japan from 1941 to 1945. The European Theatre took precedence over the Pacific and on 2 May 1945, the Third Reich fell at the hands of the Allied Powers. By this time, the death toll was enormous with almost 400,000 military deaths for the U.S. alone. In an effort to end the war with Japan quickly and avoid further loss of life, the decision to use the atomic bomb on Japan was approved. On 6 August 1945, the first atomic bomb, known as "Little Boy," was dropped on Hiroshima and three days later the second, "Fat Man," was dropped on Nagasaki. Consequently, Japan capitulated immediately and surrender ceremonies were held aboard the USS Missouri in Tokyo Bay on 2 September 1945.[105] The U.S. stood as the sole nuclear power in the world. As such, America could plausibly employ nuclear weapons against any nation without the threat of response in kind. That fact would change on 29 August 1949 with the first successful detonation of an atomic bomb by the Soviet Union; enter the age of potential nuclear war.

The immediate origins of the Cold War lie in the conflict between the Soviet Union and the West over Eastern Europe.[106] Following the collapse of Germany in 1945, each nation sought to advance its specific interests. After six long years of war France, Britain, and the Soviet Union were concerned about the balance of power and security. The U.S., as a global economic power, was interested in a world open to the free exchange of goods, money, and people.[107] As a result, the conditions for the creation of the Cold War arose in World War II out of disagreements between the Western powers

---

[105]Langer, 97.

[106]Ibid., 5.

[107]John W. Mason, *The Cold War, 1945-1991* (London: Routledge, 2007), 2.

and the Soviet Union, about what kind of postwar settlement should be made in Europe.

Although the Cold War can trace its origins to disagreements over post World War II

Europe, the reasons for its persistence and evolution go far beyond its origins. John

Mason notes that "the Cold War was not the product of one event or decision—it was the

result of a fundamental clash of ideologies and interests between the Soviet Union and

the West."[108]

Within a year of Germany's defeat, Eastern Europe was divided between the

Soviet Union and the West. With Soviet controlled governments in Poland, Bulgaria, and

Romania, and Communist parties active throughout Europe, it seemed to Western leaders

that Soviet expansion had to be countered.[109] As such, each side occupied territory in an

attempt to prevent further expansion and increase spheres of influence. The Grand

Alliance of the U.S., Great Britain, and the Soviet Union had fallen apart, and with it,

lasting hopes of a peaceful international order. Speaking at Westminster College in

Fulton, Missouri, on 5 March 1946, the former British Prime Minister Winston Churchill

said "from Stettin in the Baltic to Trieste in the Adriatic, an Iron Curtain has descended

across the Continent."[110]

The balance of power in Europe had indeed been upset with the predominance of

conventional military force favoring the Soviet Union. In 1949, Soviet Army divisions

were estimated to outnumber Western divisions at a ratio of about 125 to 14. Mason notes

---

[108]Ibid.

[109]Robert Cowley, *Cold War: A Military History* (Westminster, MD: Random House, 2005), 5-6.

[110]Ibid., 3-4.

that "it became clear to West European leaders that only the United States could ensure the balance of power in Europe."[111] Consequently, in April 1949, the North Atlantic Treaty was signed in Washington as a means to provide balance. The purpose of the North Atlantic Treaty Organization was in fact psychological. The strategic concept on which the common defense of Europe was based was simple, the ability of the U.S. to deliver the atomic bomb.[112] The U.S.' nuclear capability became the primary guarantor of peace in Europe.

The Korean War, which occurred from June 1950 to July 1953, is the third and final major event to be examined in the first historical period. After the defeat of Japan in 1945, Korea was divided at the 38th Parallel, with the Soviet Union controlling the north and the U.S. controlling the south. By 1948 North Korea was a well established communist state under the leadership of Kim Il Sung.[113] In June 1950, North Korean forces crossed the 38th Parallel and President Truman made the decision to commit U.S. forces to defend South Korea. American General Douglas MacArthur was appointed as Commander of United Nations Forces and in the early months of the war drove the North Korean forces out of the South and pushed them back to within miles of the Chinese border. This in turn provoked China to send its own forces across the Yalu River into Korea. By the end of November nearly 300,000 Chinese troops had driven United Nations troops into a long retreat that was halted just south of the 38th Parallel.[114]

---

[111]Mason, 13.

[112]Ibid.

[113]Ibid., 18.

[114]Ibid., 19-20.

Demonstrating the military feasibility and acceptability at the time, MacArthur called for the use of atomic bombs against China to stem the flow of troops into Korea. Truman denied the request and the war continued for another two years. Interestingly, soon after General Dwight D. Eisenhower took office as President of the U.S. in January 1953, he warned China indirectly through the Indian Ambassador that, unless progress was made at the peace talks at Panmunjom, the U.S. would consider using the atomic bomb against China. By the end of the decade, the nuclear option would no longer be feasible or acceptable.

The second historical period will highlight three major events: the beginning of the space race, the nuclear arms race, and the Cuban Missile Crisis. According to John Mason, "the half-decade from 1957 to 1962 has been called the 'nuclear epoch', a time when the danger of nuclear war was greater than ever before or since."[115] In relation to this study, Mason's quote is especially insightful because it emphasizes the fact that by the end of this period the U.S. could no longer employ nuclear weapons without the threat of a massive response in kind; a response so potentially devastating, that the American way of life may cease to exist.

The first major event that occurred was a spectacular scientific achievement that alarmed the U.S. because of the inherent military implications. On 4 October 1957, the Soviet Union launched the first satellite, Sputnik, into outer space, and the U.S. went into a state of shock, the Cold War enemy was suddenly ahead.[116] The implications of such a feat were distressing to Western leaders. If the Soviets had a rocket capable of putting a

[115]Ibid., 29.

[116]Zelizer, 121.

satellite into orbit they could also produce a rocket with sufficient thrust to launch an inter-continental ballistic missile with a nuclear warhead against a target in the U.S.[117] The strategic balance of power had seemingly tipped in favor of the Soviets.

The second major event, the nuclear arms race, occurred largely in response to the first. The First Secretary of the Soviet Union, Nikita Khrushchev, took immediate diplomatic advantage of the Soviets' apparent lead in missile technology. In 1958, Khrushchev attempted to separate West Germany and Britain from the North Atlantic Treaty Organization by issuing crude threats about how they could be "wiped from the face of the earth."[118] Instead of causing the North Atlantic Treaty Organization to splinter, the failed Soviet diplomatic bluff intensified the nuclear arms race under the false pretense that the U.S. suffered from a "missile gap." The nuclear arms race continued to accelerate over the coming decades. Ironically, the so called, missile gap, in favor of the Soviet Union turned out to be a myth. History later showed that the U.S. had overwhelming nuclear strategic superiority throughout the 1950s.[119]

The final major event of the second historical period was the Cuban Missile Crisis. The Cuban Missile Crisis, which occurred over a 13 day span in October 1962, is considered to be the most dangerous nuclear event of the Cold War. In the summer of 1962, Nikita Khrushchev placed strategic, intermediate-range offensive missiles on the island of Cuba, just 90 miles off the coast of Florida. Evidence of their placement was obtained by intelligence overflights from U.S. spy planes. President Kennedy

---

[117]Mason, 29.

[118]Ibid.

[119]Ibid.

immediately ordered a naval blockade and the missiles were withdrawn on 28 October.

John Mason notes the following: "the Cuban missile crisis was Khrushchev's last foreign

policy fling and it proved a disaster from which he never recovered."[120] As a result of the

Cuban Missile Crisis two key nuclear arms control treaties emerged: the Nuclear Test

Ban Treaty in 1963 and the Non-Proliferation of Nuclear Weapons Treaty in 1969. By

the end of this period, the option of nuclear war was no longer acceptable and was

avoided at all costs.

The third and final historical period for the Nuclear Age will introduce three

major historical events: the Vietnam War, the fall of the Soviet Union, and the 1991 Gulf

War. The third historical period is extremely interesting because it encompasses a time

when the specter of nuclear war still loomed, even though the idea of it has become

synonymous with "mutually assured destruction." Mason's characterization of the Cold

War is fitting for this period: "the United States and the Soviet Union clumsily engaged

in a dance of death, threatening one another with weapons that they knew must never be

used. The danger of nuclear war hung over the Cold War like a poisonous cloud of

extinction, making it a period of history like no other."[121] As a result, the U.S. had to seek

other means by which to "contain" the spread of communism.

Fearing another conflict like the Korean War, the U.S. entered the Vietnam War

incrementally. It proved to be the longest war in U.S. History. From 1954 to 1964 the

U.S. provided financial, diplomatic, and advisory support to South Vietnam. In 1965,

President Lyndon Johnson approved the decision to send combat troops, as a means to

---

[120]Ibid., 32.

[121]Ibid., x.

prevent the spread of communism to South Vietnam. America's involvement in the Vietnam War ended in 1975 when the last U.S. advisors left the country. During the war, the U.S. dropped 10 million tons of bombs on Vietnam, more than the entire amount dropped in World War II. The decision to become involved in Vietnam was later described by a top American official, George Ball, as "probably the greatest single error made by America in its history."[122]

The collapse of the Soviet Empire was the second major event for this historical period. In 1989, communism crumbled in Poland, Czechoslovakia, and East Germany; two years later, the Baltic nations of Latvia, Lithuania, and Estonia broke free from the Soviet grip, and the Ukraine voted for independence. In December 1991, the Soviet Union itself disappeared.[123] America's primary adversary, the focal point for an overwhelming majority of its national security policies, had ceased to exist. The unfathomable had occurred, and America now stood alone as the world's dominant superpower.[124]

The final major historical event to address is the 1991 Gulf War. The significance of the Gulf War in relation to this study is twofold. First, it showcases the aircraft carrier as a microinvention of nuclear fission; specifically its ability to project national military power worldwide. Second, it signals the rise of the Information Age in warfare. Iraq accused Kuwait of illegally drilling for oil in its Rumaila oil fields and subsequently

---

[122]Ibid., 33.

[123]Derek Chollet, *America Between the Wars: From 11/9 to 9/11: The Misunderstood Years Between the Fall of the Berlin Wall and the Start of the War on Terror* (New York: Public Affairs, 2009), xiii.

[124]Ibid., xiii.

demanded 10 billion dollars in reparations. Kuwait refused to pay the full 10 billion, instead offering only nine billion. As a result, Saddam Hussein ordered the invasion of Kuwait on 2 August 1990. Kuwaiti resistance to the invasion ended within a day. In response to Saddam Hussein's invasion of Kuwait, President George H. W. Bush assembled a multinational coalition to expel Iraqi Troops from the country. By January 1991, coalition naval forces were deployed in strength, based around two U.S. aircraft carriers, the Dwight D Eisenhower and Independence, and two U.S. battleships, the Wisconsin and Missouri.[125] As the buildup of forces continued, further U.S. carriers arrived in the Gulf and the Red Sea; the Midway, Theodore Roosevelt, America, Ranger and Saratoga.

The stage for the first major conflict post the Cold War was set and the world waited with great anticipation to see how the events would unfold. Operations began at 2:38 a.m. on 17 January 1991, when Task Force Normandy, with eight US AH-64 Apache helicopters, led by two MH-53 Pave Low helicopters, destroyed Iraqi radar sites near the Iraq–Saudi Arabia border.[126] Five hours after the first attacks, Baghdad state radio broadcast a voice identified as Saddam Hussein's declaring: "The great duel, the mother of all battles, has begun. The dawn of victory nears as this great showdown begins." After a month of intense aerial bombardment, General Norman Schwarzkopf initiated the ground assault of Operation Desert Storm on 23 February 1991. Within 100 hours, the Iraqi Army suffered a humiliating defeat at the hands of the American

---

[125]Jonathon Riley, *Decisive Battles: From Yorktown to Operation Desert Storm* (London: Continuum International Publishing, 2010), 212.

[126]Ibid., 217.

coalition. Jonathon Riley, in his book *Decisive Battles: From Yorktown to Operation Desert Storm*, describes the battle:

> After all the preparation and long build-up, the actual operation was something of an anti-climax. The Coalition ground advance was much swifter than anyone had expected. On 26 February, the Iraqis began to withdraw from Kuwait; a long column of retreating troops . . . this was subjected to such extensive attack by coalition forces that the road, littered with burned-out vehicles and the bodies of the dead and wounded, became known as the Highway of Death.[127]

Thanks to the advent of mass media, millions of people around the world watched in amazement as the events unfolded before them in near real-time. The technological advantage displayed by the U.S. Military was truly astonishing. Information flowed faster than ever before, providing the American coalition an overwhelming operational advantage. As a result, the American coalition crushed the fourth largest army in the world in just over a month. A post war assessment of the conflict revealed the following: the Iraqis had 20,000 killed, 75,000 wounded and 80,000 prisoners taken during the campaign, compared with only 190 Coalition killed and 75 wounded, many the result of accidents or friendly fire.[128]

With the historical context of the Nuclear Age established, the study will now begin analysis of its key concepts: the emergence of a strategic resource dependent macroinvention, the techno-resource-dependence transition period, how the U.S. ensured availability and access to the resource, and subsequent influence on national security policy. As with the previous two chapters, each of the four narrative questions will be

---

[127]Ibid., 221.

[128]Ibid., 222.

used to guide the analysis.[129] The historical experience of the U.S. will be taken into direct account as each question is examined. Of note, the study will periodically expand its scope to provide greater clarity and understanding.

What new strategic resource dependent technology emerged that had a direct impact on the U.S.' ability to wage war? For the Nuclear Age, the macroinvention, nuclear fission, was a process enabled by technological invention. In this regard, the macroinvention for the Nuclear Age differs substantially from the previous two examples. This differentiation is important, because of its potential implications for preliminary analysis of the Information Age, whereby the Internet may be viewed as the premier macroinvention of the age.

The study will now briefly examine the origins of nuclear fission in an effort to shed light on how it affected warfare in the twentieth century. The science of atomic radiation, atomic change, and nuclear fission was developed from 1895 to 1945, much of it in the last six years of that period. Nuclear Fission was first discovered accidentally, on 21 December 1938 in Nazi Germany, by German radio chemists Otto Hahn and Fritz Strassmann. The discovery was made a full nine months before the beginning of World War II. Hahn brooded on the probable military applications of his discovery and seriously considered suicide. It was a discovery that in the long run would sharply limit national

---

[129]Four narrative questions: What new Strategic resource dependent technology emerged that had a direct impact on the nation's ability to wage war? What was the associated Strategic resource(s) that allowed the production, sustainment, and operation of this new technology and what was the level of access? How did the nation employ its military instrument of national power to ensure access to the strategic resource(s)? What national security policy changes were made as a result of this new technology and the associated strategic resource?

sovereignty and change forever the relationship between nation-states.[130] One of the most influential macroinventions in human history had been created, and it came as a complete surprise.

From 1939 to 1945 the science of nuclear fission accelerated dramatically under the Manhattan Project, as development was focused on what is easily the most influential microinvention of this chapter, the atomic bomb. After the rise of the Nazi Party in 1933, dozens of German scientists began fleeing the country; many of whom sought asylum in the U.S. and Britain. Two scientists in particular, Rudolf Peierls and Otto Frisch, arrived in England in 1937 and 1939 respectively. While working at the University of Birmingham in England in 1940, the two scientists co-authored a memorandum detailing the constructive properties and implications of building an atomic bomb. In her book, *Remembering the Manhattan Project: Perspectives on the Making of the Atomic Bomb and Its Legacy*, Cynthia Kelly notes the following: "the Frisch-Peierls Memorandum must rank as one of the most historic documents of the twentieth century." Kelly goes on to highlight that the memorandum was written at a time when the war was still confined to Europe and the Soviets, the Japanese, and the Americans were all interested bystanders but had not yet entered the war.[131] The key points of the Frisch-Peierls Memorandum were:

> 1. As a weapon, the super-bomb would be practically irresistible. There is no
>
> material or structure that could be expected to resist the force of the explosion.

---

[130]Cynthia C. Kelly, *Remembering the Manhattan Project: Perspectives on the Making of the Atomic Bomb and Its Legacy* (River Edge, NJ: World Scientific Publishing Co., 2005), 17.

[131]Ibid., 44.

2. Owing to the spreading of radioactive substances with the wind, the bomb

could probably not be used without killing large numbers of civilians, and this

may make it unsuitable as a weapon for use by this [Britain] country.

3. We have no information that the same idea has also occurred to other scientists

but since all the theoretical data bearing on this problem are published, it is

quite conceivable that Germany is, in fact, developing this weapon.[132]

In spite of the implications set forth in the second key point of the Frisch-Peierls

Memorandum, the Americans increased their efforts to build the atomic bomb; with the

first and third points of the memorandum providing the impetus for doing so. With a

heightened sense of urgency and concerns for security, the U.S. Army took over process

development, engineering design, procurement of materials, and site selection for pilot

plants for four methods of making fissionable material in June 1942.[133] Three years later,

on 16 July 1945, the first successful test of an atomic device, codenamed "Trinity," took

place at Alamogordo in New Mexico. Upon seeing the explosion of the Trinity test, the

following ancient verse from the 2,000 year old Bhagavad Gita flashed into Robert

Oppenheimer's mind: "If the radiance of a thousand suns were to burst forth at once in

the sky, that would be like the splendor of the Mighty One. I am become death, The

Scatterer of Worlds."[134]

---

[132]Ibid., 44-45.

[133]World Nuclear Association, "Online History of Nuclear Energy," updated June 2010, http://www.world-nuclear.org/info/inf54.html (accessed 28 September 2012).

[134]Langer, 248.

Another significant microinvention, naval nuclear propulsion, emerged in the latter half of the second historical period.[135] At a time when the strategic balance of power had seemingly tipped in favor of the Soviets with the launch of Sputnik, thereby accelerating the nuclear arms race, the Eisenhower Administration was desperately seeking ways to gain an advantage in ballistic missile delivery. The Navy had been essentially frozen out of the Manhattan Project, which the Army had taken over in 1942, because of a conflict an Admiral had with the scientists who were helping to organize the effort to mobilize civilian science. As such, it lacked a viable weapon platform with which to challenge the nuclear weapon dominance that the newly created Air Force had in the early years of the Cold War[136] In an effort to gain a significant role in the sponsorship of nuclear weapons, the U.S. Navy developed their own ballistic missile delivery program, "Polaris."

Polaris was essentially the U.S. Navy's development program of the solid-fueled Polaris missile and its associated submarine system. It gained approval and funding in 1956 and four years later the first Polaris Armed Nuclear Submarine, the USS George Washington, went to sea.[137] The strategic advantages offered by nuclear powered submarines were tremendous. They were difficult to counter, highly mobile, stealthy, and therefore hard to locate and track. In addition, they could stay submerged for months at a time with unlimited range, thanks to nuclear propulsion. Lethality continually increased

---

[135] As defined in chapter 3, the Nuclear Age: 1954 to 1962.

[136] Henry D. Sokolski, "Getting MAD: Nuclear Mutual Assured Destruction, its Origins, and Practice" (Strategic Studies Institute, November 2004), 123-125.

[137] Ibid., 126.

throughout the Cold War as the Polaris missiles were eventually upgraded to "Poseidon" missiles in 1972, and later, during the 1980s, upgraded again with "Trident" missiles. The direct impact that these microinventions had on the U.S.' ability to wage war were astounding: one Trident Nuclear Submarine carried more fire power than all the bombs dropped in World War II.[138]

Capitalizing on the inherent advantages of nuclear propulsion, the U.S. Navy introduced its newest class of aircraft carriers, the "Nimitz" Class, a year later. In 1961, the USS Enterprise was commissioned as the world's first nuclear powered aircraft carrier. The Enterprise played a key role in the naval blockade of the Cuban Missile Crisis and supported combat operations in both Vietnam and the 1991 Gulf War. Nuclear propulsion had effectively eliminated one of the most problematic conditions of carrier warfare, the need to refuel at sea. Thus, the U.S.' ability to project military power around the world was greatly increased.

Having explored the macroinvention and subsequent microinventions of the Nuclear Age, the study will now direct its focus to the second narrative question: what was the associated strategic resource that allowed the production, sustainment, and operation of the microinventions derived from nuclear fission, and what was the U.S.' level of access? Like the internal combustion engine in the previous chapter, there are numerous resources associated with the production, sustainment, and operation of the microinventions derived from nuclear fission. However, this study will focus on uranium as the strategic resource, because of its inherent ability to make the process of nuclear fission possible.

---

[138]Mason, x.

67

The history of uranium can be traced back to Germany in the sixteenth century. At that time, silver was found in a river in the mountainous region near Saxony. Jeremy Bernstein, in his book *Plutonium: A History of the World's Most Dangerous Element*, details its discovery: as the silver boom ebbed and flowed, mining continued into the eighteenth century and the miners eventually encountered a shiny black mineral that they called "pitchblende." He goes on to note that it was first analyzed by a self-educated chemist named Martin Klaproth, and in 1789, he found in it what he called a "strange kind of half metal" that seemed to be a new element.[139] In admiration and honor of his countryman William Herschel, who was credited with discovering the planet Uranus, Klaproth decided to call the element uran. The name later became "uranium."

Uranium was discovered in other locations across Germany throughout the eighteenth century, but at the time it was considered useless. However, in 1841, the French chemist Eugene Peligot, experimenting with uranium, found that he could make it into a metal as dense as gold. In addition, it was also learned that uranium salts and oxides could be used to produce wonderfully colored ceramics.[140] This fact caught the attention of Wilhelm Conrad Rontgen who was a professor of physics at the University of Wurzburg in Germany. At the time, Rontgen had been experimenting with what were known as Crookes tubes (glass cones from which the air had been pumped out). Bernstein describes the moment in which uranium first gained scientific significance: "curious, Rontgen held various materials between himself and the screen and much to his

---

[139]Jeremy Bernstein, *Plutonium: A History of the World's Most Dangerous Element* (Washington, DC: Joseph Henry Press, 2007), 3.

[140]Ibid., 19.

astonishment saw the bones of his hand. He called the mysterious beam 'x-rays' and persuaded his wife to have her hand x-rayed."[141] It quickly became understood that x-rays were a new medical diagnostic tool of immense importance—uranium was no longer just a useless mineral.

During the latter half of the nineteenth century research surrounding the properties of uranium increased and by December 1903, the nature of the radiation had been at least partially clarified. Four elements; uranium, thorium, radium, and polonium, were then known to be "radioactive."[142] Because it seemed that uranium was the source of a seemingly limitless supply of energy, scientists desperately continued their research in an attempt to figure what was emanating from it. In 1905, German Physicist Albert Einstein provided the answer. Einstein concluded that "the residues of the decay have less mass than the parent object that decays. This mass difference supplies the needed energy through the relation $E=mc^2$."[143] Research on the curious metal and its radioactive properties continued over the next two decades and on 21 December 1938, with the discovery of nuclear fission, uranium became one of the deadliest elements in the world.

In his book, *Uranium Matters: Central European Uranium in International Politics, 1900-1960*, Zbynek Zemab states that "in the race for the nuclear weapon, availability of uranium ore was of the essence."[144] In a letter written on 2 August 1939,

---

[141]Ibid., 19-20.

[142]Ibid., 21.

[143]Ibid., 22.

[144]Zbynek A. B. Zemab, *Uranium Matters: Central European Uranium in International Politics, 1900-1960* (New York: Central European University Press, 2008), 19.

Albert Einstein warned President Roosevelt of the destructive potential of nuclear fission and the subsequent importance of the uranium mines at Jáchymov, which had come under Nazi control. In response, Roosevelt established a Uranium Commission in October 1939, to determine the feasibility of building an atomic bomb.[145] Determining the availability of uranium ore and gaining access to it became the critical first steps. As it turned out, gaining access to uranium was a relatively easy but expensive task with much of the uranium needed for the Manhattan Project obtained in the Belgian Congo. General Groves secured a monopoly over the purchase and processing of uranium world wide by 3 December 1945. Through the establishment of the Combined Development Trust, a joint British-American Government Agency, controlled by Groves, the U.S. had cornered 97 percent of the world's production of uranium.[146]

Unlike oil in the previous example, uranium turned out to be a relatively abundant resource. Zemab explains that after the hectic growth of the uranium industry in the 1950s, the development of the sector took a more peaceful course in the 1960s. Uranium ore was no longer in short supply and the potential for using it for peaceful purposes quickly emerged.[147] He further notes that military plutonium, derived from uranium ore, is a fixed target because all of its producers (with the exception of North Korea) have declared that they are no longer producing plutonium for weapons. Most of the producing countries presumably have all that they could conceivably ever need. As such, production was suspended in the U.S. during the 1990s.

---

[145]Ibid., 5.

[146]Ibid., 19.

[147]Ibid., 273.

The study now turns to the third narrative question: how did the U.S. employ its military instrument of national power to ensure access to uranium? In short, it never really had to. Instead, the U.S. employed economic, diplomatic, and informational instruments of national power, the latter two enhanced by its nuclear capability, to prevent other countries from gaining access to it. Gar Alperovitz in his book, *The Decision to Use the Atomic Bomb and the Architecture of an American Myth*, argues that the U.S. dropped the bomb on Japan mainly as a demonstration of its military power to the Soviet Union, and subsequently, was able to use it as a diplomatic lever to wring concessions from the Soviet Union in Eastern Europe.[148] Whether or not Alperovitz's claim is correct is a matter of greater historical debate and beyond the scope of this study. His claim does however illuminate the fact that the U.S. enjoyed increased diplomatic power, thanks to the advent of the nuclear bomb.

The study will now focus on the fourth and final narrative question: what national security policy changes did the U.S. make as a result of this new technology and the associated strategic resource? The emergence of nuclear fission and its associated microinventions indeed reshaped the concept of modern warfare. At the time when World War II had just ended, America emerged as the world's sole nuclear power, and the Grand Alliance was falling apart over disputes about the future of Europe, U.S. Foreign Policy was in a state of confusion and lacked focus. Ironically, within a few years the start of the Cold War provided it the focus it needed, an ideological war backed by the threat of nuclear weapons.

---

[148]Gar Alperovitz, *The Decision to Use the Atomic Bomb and the Architecture of an American Myth* (New York: Random House, 1995), 5-6.

U.S. national security policy, during the Nuclear Age, underwent multiple adaptations and revisions in response to the emergence of nuclear fission and its associated microinventions, most importantly the atomic bomb. Not surprisingly, national security policy in the Nuclear Age centered on the feasibility and acceptability of using nuclear weapons. An attempt to examine all of the adaptations and revisions that U.S. national security policy underwent during the Nuclear Age is beyond the intent and scope of this study. Therefore, the study will focus on core national security policy in relation to the feasibility and acceptability of using nuclear weapons, specifically the core policy for of each of the three historical periods.[149]

During the first period, 1939 to 1953, it was both feasible and acceptable to employ nuclear weapons without the threat of catastrophic response in kind. During the second period, 1954 to 1963, the option to use nuclear weapons was still feasible, but the acceptability of their use was greatly reduced. This was in light of the fact, that unless the U.S. successfully struck first, there would be a near catastrophic response in kind by the Soviet Union. By the third period, 1964 to 1992, with the fear that the use of nuclear weapons would result in nuclear holocaust, the option was no longer acceptable. As such, the U.S. avoided their use at all costs. The core U.S. national security policies that surfaced during the three historical periods were the policies of containment, limited war, and mutually assured destruction. Each of these policies wrestled with the challenges of Soviet deterrence and nuclear counter-proliferation.

---

[149]Three historical periods: 1939 to 1953 (the end of the Korean War), 1954 to 1962 (the Cuban missile crisis), and 1963 to 1992 (one year passed the fall of the Soviet Union).

The U.S. began to take a more aggressive stance towards the Soviet Union in 1946 over disputes about the future of Europe, and the perceived threat of communist ideology. John Mason noted that in 1945, Congress was dominated by Republicans intent on reducing military spending, now that the war in Europe was over and in light of the fact that America stood as the only atomic power in the world. As such, the U.S. began to demobilize, reducing its forces from 12 million to 3 million in one year.[150] Many politicians thought that America's atomic power alone was sufficient enough to deter the communist expansion. However, since Soviet Army divisions outnumbered Western divisions at a ratio of about 125 to 14, the decision to demobilize so many forces so quickly weakened the U.S.' bargaining power. To make matters worse, no one knew exactly how to gain diplomatic advantage out of America's nuclear monopoly.[151] This conundrum was one of the primary reasons for why the U.S.' Foreign Policy seemed to be in a "state of confusion" during the latter half of the 1940s.

As the U.S. tried to figure out its foreign policy, a debate over what exactly was the source of Soviet expansion emerged. George F. Kennan, a well known political theorist and historian at the time, suggested that the of source of expansion may indeed be a result of conditions inside the Soviet Union itself, and not in response to what happened outside of it. Mason describes the seriousness of Kennan's theory: "the implications of Kennan's analysis were chilling" because, if they were in fact true, "then no action taken by the United States would diminish Soviet hostility towards the West." He goes on to note that in light of this, "Kennan recommended a policy that can be summed up in one

---

[150]Mason, 5.

[151]Ibid., 8.

73

word—'containment.' Containment was essentially a policy of the middle way, between isolationism on the one hand and preventative war on the other."[152] Acknowledging the implications of Kennan's analysis, the Truman Administration officially adopted the policy of containment in 1947.

U.S. Foreign Policy continued to struggle with how to best deter Soviet aggression for the rest of the 1940s. Then, in April 1950, just two months before the start of the Korean War, the State and Defense Departments produced the highly ideological document, National Security Council (NSC) 68. NSC 68 held that U.S. survival depended on building a successful political-economic system in the free world, constructing defenses able to deter attack, and fighting limited wars to impose U.S. terms.[153] It advocated development of vast stores of nuclear weapons and powerful conventional forces led by a U.S. alliance with other Western nations by arguing that there was an imbalance of power between "free" and "slave" states, free being those under Western influence and slave being those under Soviet influence. As such, it stated that the U.S. needed to increase its military forces massively so that it could respond to any Soviet challenge at the level of that threat.[154] After the onset of the Korean War, President Truman approved NSC 68. Thus, the U.S. began to once again increase its military forces to contain the threat of communism in Korea.

---

[152]Ibid.

[153]Andrew J. Bacevich, *Long War: A History of U. S. National Security Policy Since World War II* (New York: Columbia University Press, 2009), xxvi.

[154]Meena Bose, *Shaping and Signaling Presidential Policy: The National Security Decision Making of Eisenhower and Kennedy* (College Station, TX: Texas A&M University Press, 1998), 6.

National security policy underwent further adaptation under the Eisenhower

Administration in 1953 with the New Look Policy. The basic premise of the New Look

was that the U.S. should rely on its superiority in naval and air power, and particularly its

nuclear capability, rather than count on ground forces to deter communist advances

around the world.[155] Interestingly, national security policy returned to the basic principles

of NSC 68 in the early 1960s under the Kennedy administration's policy of Flexible

Response. Kennedy asserted that the U.S. should be able to respond to Soviet actions on a

variety of levels below the nuclear threshold. As such, he told the nation during the

Berlin Crisis in the summer of 1961, "We intend to have a wider choice than humiliation

or all-out nuclear action."[156]

The Korean War was extremely influential because it "abruptly ended the

incoherence of American foreign policy in the years 1946 to 1950" and set a "precedent

for fighting a limited war in the nuclear age."[157] In 1951, America's national security

policy was dominated by the belief that the "world was so closely interconnected that a

communist victory anywhere would threaten vital US interests." [158] Consequently, the

U.S. continued its war in Korea for another two years and on 27 July 1953, with the

signing of the armistice, successfully prevented the spread of communism to South

Korea. Most importantly, stopping the spread of communism to South Korea was

---

[155]Ibid.

[156]Bose, 6.

[157]Ibid., 22.

[158]Ibid.

achieved without the use of nuclear weapons; thus setting a precedent for future national security policy.

After the Korean War, U.S. national security policy still faced two problems: containing the spread of communism and deterring nuclear war. The concept of limited war offered an answer. Herman Kahn, a leading military strategist and game theorist, conducted some of the earliest work on the concept of limited war. Kahn argued that nuclear war was survivable, and as such, the U.S. should acquire the limited war capacity needed to survive it.[159] This entailed integrating conventional forces into the overall policy of deterrence. Radhika Withana, in his book *Power, Politics, Law: International Law and State Behavior During International Crises*, explained that "limited war was a strategy aimed to augment the deterrence posture by providing the means to fight a war in a way which did not automatically involve suicide via nuclear war."[160] The policy of limited war was adopted by the U.S. in the early 1960s and later influenced America's decision to enter Vietnam.

Even though the policy of limited war emerged in the early 1960s, the Cuban Missile Crisis of 1962 demonstrated that general nuclear war was still a possibility. Largely due to the nuclear arms race of the 1950s, both the U.S. and the Soviet Union possessed enough nuclear weapons to achieve near catastrophic destruction of one another by 1963. Subsequently, policy makers sought ways to enhance nuclear deterrence. Withana noted that nuclear deterrence relates not just to the protection of a

---

[159]Ibid., 31-32.

[160]Radhika Withana, *Power, Politics, Law: International Law and State Behavior During International Crises* (Leiden: Martinus Nijhoff Publishers, 2008), 31.

State's own defense, but also to actual threats of military retaliation in defense of a third State party.[161] This meant that the U.S. had to deter nuclear war throughout Europe as well as against America itself.

In response to the need to provide nuclear deterrence on two different continents, studies of political and military strategy, influenced by game theory, examined the intricacies of deterrence and limited war. They concluded that, in the nuclear age, a policy of mutually assured destruction was the most viable means of deterrence. Keir Lieber defined mutually assured destruction as "a doctrine of military strategy and national security policy in which a full-scale use of high-yield weapons of mass destruction by two opposing sides would effectively result in the complete, utter, and irrevocable annihilation of both the attacker and the defender."[162] During the Johnson Administration 1963 to 1969, then Secretary of Defense, Robert McNamara, enshrined Mutually Assured Destruction as "official" U.S. policy for nuclear deterrence.[163]

What conclusions can be drawn from the U.S.' example in the Nuclear Age? Interestingly, the U.S.' example offered very unique insights into every aspect of the study's framework.[164] It would be conceivable to draw multiple insights from every aspect. However, exploring every possible insight would greatly expand the scope of this

---

[161]Ibid.

[162]Keir A. Lieber, "The Rise of U.S. Nuclear Primacy," *Foreign Affairs* 85, no. 2 (March/April 2006): 42-54.

[163]Sokolski, 279.

[164]The emergence of a strategic resource dependent macroinvention and subsequent microinventions, the associated strategic resource, the techno-resource-dependent transition period, and affects on national security policy.

study. Therefore, the study will focus only on what it deemed the most salient insight for each aspect.

The first pertains to the macroinvention, nuclear fission. Unlike the previous examples, the macroinvention in the Nuclear Age was just as much a process as it was a technological invention. This distinction is important for two reasons. First, in the greater concept of resource conflict, the macroinvention in this case overshadowed the importance of the strategic resource. That is, nuclear fission, due to its inherent military implications, was not readily shared with other nations. Therefore, it was inconsequential whether or not a nation had access to uranium, as long as it did not understand or could not perform the process of nuclear fission. Because neither the steam engine nor the internal combustion engine shared this profound military implication, they were readily shared with other nations. Hence, conflict during the Age of Oil focused on the resource itself and not the whether or not a nation possessed the knowledge to build internal combustion engines. The second reason has to do with what this study will argue is a significant macroinvention in the Information Age, the Internet. Similar to nuclear fission, the Internet, when viewed as a macroinvention, is a synthesis of many technological inventions, as opposed to the examples given in the Age of Steam and the Age of Oil.

The second insight concerns the strategic resource, uranium. Initially, the availability and level of access the U.S. had to uranium were unknown. Once availability and level of access were known to some degree, the U.S. sought to control, and therefore limit, the distribution of it via economic means. That is, unlike Germany's example, the U.S. sought to "prevent" access vice acquire it, during the latter half of the 1940s. This

78

distinction raises interesting questions, especially since uranium was in overabundance by the end of the Nuclear Age. Are there diplomatic negatives to controlling or preventing access to a strategic resource? At what point does it become too costly to use economic power? What is the threshold for applying national military power to prevent or acquire access to a strategic resource? To be sure, these questions are not new. They are however, worth considering as the U.S. moves deeper into the twenty-first century.

The third insight centers on the incredibly short duration of the techno-resource-dependence transition period.[165] Nuclear fission was discovered on 21 December 1938 and Albert Einstein informed President Roosevelt of the importance of the uranium mines at Jachymov on 2 August 1939, just eight months later. Furthermore, General Groves secured a monopoly over the purchase and processing of uranium world wide by 3 December 1945. These factors, coupled with the eventual overabundance of uranium, effectively negated the techno-resource-dependence transition period. This brings to light two very important realities: the emergence of a macroinvention that is dependent on a strategic resource may not lead to prolonged resource dependence or resource dependence at all. These realities appear overly straight forward on the surface. However, there is potential for policy makers to overreact in the face of perceived finite resources.

The final insight, and perhaps the most intriguing in light of the Information Age, revolves around national security policy. The policies of containment and limited war, discussed in the first and second historical periods respectively, are especially thought

---

[165]Techno-resource-dependence transition period: The period between the emergence of a macroinvention and the point whereby a nation consciously assumes a level of dependence on this technology and its associated resource to sustain and/ or enhance an instrument of national power.

provoking when considering the prospect of cyber warfare in the twenty-first century. As the sole nuclear power, post World War II, the U.S. had to adopt a policy that both protected its allies, while simultaneously dissuaded them from producing the means to build nuclear weapons. In addition, the U.S. had to confront adversaries in such a way that it did not provoke an all out nuclear war. Currently, the U.S. is not the only cyber-power in the world. However, it may achieve preeminent cyber warfare capabilities within the next 25 to 50 years. Should the U.S. attempt to dissuade allies from developing advanced cyber warfare capabilities under the auspice that it will protect them instead? How would such a notion be received? Could there be such a thing as "limited" cyber warfare? What would it look like and what would be its threshold before invoking all out war? How would it fit into national security policy? Would a policy of cyber counter-proliferation be possible? These questions may seem outlandish, but then again, in 1937, so did the notion that one bomb could destroy an entire city.

CHAPTER 5

CONCLUSIONS AND CONSIDERATIONS FOR NATIONAL

SECURITY POLICY IN THE INFORMATION AGE

The purpose of this study was to examine technological strategic resource

dependence, its potential for conflict in the twenty-first century, and subsequent

influences on U.S. national security policy. In particular, the study explored whether or

not the notion that nations were in a constant state of, or preparing for, armed conflict

over strategic resources—specifically those linked to critical technologies that sustained

economic prosperity and national security—is substantiated. To gain insight, the study

explored five interrelated concepts within the context of three historical examples.[166] The

study did not find the expected conclusion with regards to historical strategic resource

conflict. That is, it did not find that technological strategic resource dependence always

led to "armed" conflict; nor were nations in a constant state of, or preparing for, armed

conflict over strategic resources. Instead, the study found that strategic resource

dependence more often than not led to economic and informational conflict; with

informational conflict increasing as technology progressed. More precisely, emergent

technology tended to have a much greater and longer lasting influence on policy, which

in turn shaped conflict, than the resource itself. The study will now turn to analysis and

considerations for the Information Age.

---

[166]Five interrelated concepts: macroinventions/microinventions, strategic
resources and access, usage of instruments of national power—specifically military,
effects on national security policy, and the concept of techno—resource—dependence
transition periods. Three historical examples: Britain during the Age of Steam, Germany
during the Age of Oil, and the United States in the Nuclear Age.

Chapter 5 will generally follow the same format used in the previous chapters. First, it will briefly define the Information Age and introduce relevant characteristics to provide analytical context. Second, it will address each of the four narrative questions in relation to the Information Age, to guide analysis and generate considerations.[167] Insights gained from the three historical examples will be woven into the analysis whenever possible, to provide strength and clarity. Third, generated considerations will be explored to see how they might influence U.S. national security policy over the next 25 to 50 years. The chapter will conclude with final thoughts and recommendations for future research.

Historical bookends for the Information Age have not yet been established by the academic community. This is primarily because we are currently in the middle of it and because debate continues between economists, historians, and scientists, and over what should be considered the actual start of the Information Age. Mark Burgin, in his book *Theory of Information: Fundamentality, Diversity and Unification*, states "it is generally acknowledged that we have been living in the information age, at least, since the middle of the 20th century."[168] This view takes into account the launch of Sputnik in October 1957, and the "space race" that ensued. Others speculate that the Information Age,

---

[167]Four narrative questions: What new strategic resource dependent technology emerged that had a direct impact on the nation's ability to wage war? What was the associated strategic resource(s) that allowed the production, sustainment, and operation of this new technology and what was the level of access? How did the nation employ its military instrument of national power to ensure access to the strategic resource(s)? What national security policy changes were made as a result of this new technology and the associated strategic resource?

[168]Mark Burgin, *Theory of Information: Fundamentality, Diversity and Unification* (Hackensack, NJ: World Scientific Publishing Co., 2009), v.

commonly referred to as the "information revolution," really began in the 1970s when digital communications began to affect the global economy. Not surprisingly, this view is widely held among economists. Yet another group, mostly comprised of the information technology and social science communities, points to the mid 1990s as a possible start point due to the rise of the Internet and it's affects on technology and society in general. Suffice to say, the official start of the Information Age is still being decided.

On the other hand, the general characteristics of the Information Age are not in debate. These characteristics include a more globalized economy, increased contact between individuals, groups, and nations, and added reliance on digital communications. Indeed, with the advent of digital interconnectedness, many aspects of society that were previously semi-compartmentalized have now become intertwined, and therefore interdependent, on digital technology. For example, the provision of food, shelter, infrastructure, transportation, communications, health care, and even defense are now largely digitally interdependent.[169] Although it remains beyond the scope and intent of this study to examine all characteristics of the Information Age, the study must acknowledge them to establish context. Given that, the study will focus on unique characteristics of the Information Age that pertain directly to the use of national military power and its potential influence on national security policy.

One of the more unique characteristics of the Information Age that will influence national security policy is the threat of cyber warfare. According to the U.S. *National Security Strategy* of 2010, "cyber security threats represent one of the most serious

---

[169]Committee on Critical Mineral Impacts of the U.S. Economy, *Minerals, Critical Minerals, and the U.S. Economy* (Washington, DC: National Academies Press, 2008), 36.

national security, public safety, and economic challenges we face as a nation."[170]

Countering this threat poses substantial challenges. Major James Coughlin, a cyber warfare officer with the U.S. Air force, notes that "instead of having to deal with a few near-peer competitors like the other domains, in cyberspace the peer competitors are national, non-state actors, contractors, and even twelve year olds who know how to use a search engine and write scripts."[171] To make matters worse, the act of obfuscation (intentionally hiding or creating confusion) in cyber warfare makes it hard to determine where a cyber attack originated or by whom. This is especially alarming given the fact that many of our defense systems; communications, navigation, automated function, and information collection and dissemination, are almost entirely interdependent on digital technology.

With the analytical context for the Information Age established, the study will now turn its focus to the first narrative question: what new strategic resource dependent technology emerged that had a direct impact on the nation's ability to wage war? For the Information Age the Internet serves as the premier macroinvention. Myriam Cavelty described the Internet as "a global decentralized communication network of computer networks."[172] This interconnected network enabled the U.S. to simultaneously harness and synchronize all instruments of national power; diplomatic, informational, military,

_____

[170]White House, *National Security Strategy* (Washington, DC: Government Printing Office, 2010), 27.

[171]James R. Coughlin, "What are Cyberspace Operations?" (Master's Thesis, Command and General Staff College, Fort Leavenworth, KS, 2012), 2.

[172]Myriam D. Cavelty, *Power and Security in the Information Age* (Abingdon, Oxon: Ashgate Publishing Group, 2008), 17.

and economic, thereby strengthening the linkage between strategic policy and tactical operations. The Internet also generated numerous microinventions that improved military operations. Examples include personal data assistants, voice-over-internet-protocol communications, and digital full motion video used by drones. The advent of these microinventions increased the efficiency and precision of military communications, navigation, and targeting. In many cases, these were a direct result of the experiences of the 1991 Gulf War.

The study will now apply insights garnered from the three historical periods to the Internet as the premier macroinvention of the Information Age. The first is that the Internet is similar to the steam engine, in the fact that it increased capability across all aspects of national power, while simultaneously increasing technological dependence. Furthermore, it had unforeseen societal and economic effects that ultimately affected the national security policy, specifically, it increased national and social contact and increased economic interdependence in the global economy. The insight from the Age of Oil that can be applied to the Information Age is that, forethought must be given as to how best to employ a new technology within the current and expected security environment. The insight that can be brought forward from the Nuclear Age is that macroinvention, specifically the capabilities, overshadows the importance of the resource because the technology is so diffuse and the resources are relatively abundant. In this regard the Internet is a truly unique macroinvention that poses significant challenges for national security policy in the twenty-first century.

The study now turns to the second narrative question: what was the associated strategic resource(s) that allowed the production, sustainment, and operation of the

Internet and what was the level of access? There are numerous resources associated with the production of computers—the primary technology that comprises the Internet. Among them are aluminum, antimony, barium, cadmium, chromium, copper, gold, iron, lead, mercury, platinum, and zinc to name a few. Although most of these resources are relatively common, access to many of them are secured economically from other nations around the world. Furthermore, production resources are used up rather quickly with little return. The National Resources Defense Council notes that "the sheer volume of waste generated to make a typical desktop computer is staggering: more than 500 pounds of fossil fuels alone are guzzled up—several times the weight of your computer—not to mention nearly 50 pounds of chemicals, and 1.5 tons of water."[173] Within a globalized economy, this creates a situation similar to Britain's experience during the Age of Steam whereby, economic dependence required that resources flowed freely, many of which did so by maritime means.

Although most of the resources associated with the Internet are common, some are considered critical because there is little or no access within the U.S. They must be imported from other countries which increases our dependence on the globalized market. In light of this, maintaining access to critical mineral resources has become an important issue for national security.[174] Based on use and availability, the Committee on Critical Mineral Impacts of the U.S. Economy determined that the following minerals resources are of critical importance: copper, gallium, indium, lithium, manganese, niobium,

[173]National Resources Defense Council, "Your Computer's Lifetime Journey," http://www.nrdc.org/living/stuff/your-computers-lifetime-journey.asp (accessed 16 November 2012).

[174]Committee on Critical Mineral Impacts of the U.S. Economy, 42.

platinum group metals, rare earth elements, tantalum, titanium, and vanadium.[175] The committee also concluded that "all minerals and mineral products could be or could become critical to some degree, depending on their importance and availability" and that many are "an essential input for a national priority, such as national defense or industry, or may be important to a region or the nation as a whole."[176] In short, even though the resources of the Information Age are in relative abundance, they have become a critical commodity because they are widely used and must be obtained from the global market.

The study will now address the third narrative question: how should the U.S. employ its military instrument of national power to ensure access to the strategic resource(s)? In light of the characteristics of the Information Age and the first two narrative questions, there are three considerations for how the U.S. should employ its military instrument of national power to ensure access to the strategic resources. First, just like the British did during the Age of Steam, the U.S. Navy should be bolstered and employed to enhance collective maritime security, especially in light of the fact that our dependence on critical mineral resources will likely increase. Second, the U.S. should avoid overreliance on the military instrument of national power to secure access to associated resources. Currently this does not seem to be a problem. When it is necessary, as many instruments of national power as possible should be employed to mitigate unwanted second and third order effects. The third is that the U.S. should tailor its cyber warfare abilities to the security environment and coordinate use with allies. Doing so may

---

[175]Ibid., 222.

[176]Ibid., 223.

help avoid a potential "cyber arms race" which in turn, may exponentially increase critical mineral resource values and complicate access.

The study will now address the final narrative question: what national security policy changes should be made as a result of this new technology and the associated strategic resource? The inherent interconnectedness of the Information Age makes this is an extremely complicated question. So much so that it generates additional questions: does policy guide resource conflict or does resource conflict guide policy? Are historical policies applicable to the Information Age—can there be a policy of containment or limited cyber warfare? This question is perhaps best answered by looking back at history to see what worked and what did not. As an island nation, Britain's "two power standard" seemed a worthy goal for maintaining maritime security.[177] In the Information Age U.S national security policy should seek to do the same with regards to cyber warfare capabilities. This would help ensure prosperity and security across all national power domains. Germany's example offers two insights for national security change. First, early identification of the techno-resource-dependence transition period allowed them to enact national security policies to increase access to vital strategic resources. Second, it allowed them to overcome relative shortages by seeking alternatives. The U.S. should emulate this with both current and future emergent technologies.

There are three final conclusions to discuss before turning to future research recommendations. Each is of a broader sense for the Information Age in particular. The first is that information as a commodity within itself has risen in value during the

---

[177]This standard called for the Royal Navy to maintain a number of battleships at least equal to the combined strength of the next two largest navies in the world.

Information Age. The Committee on Critical Mineral Impacts of the U.S. Economy noted that "in the information age, information is becoming the major resource of power. The notion of soft power, for example, rests on the contention that power is passing from the capital-rich to the information-rich."[178] In this regard, the value of information as a critical resource continues to increase. The second conclusion is that the macroinvention generates the primary resource of the age "information." This is especially intriguing because it is the only macroinvention discussed in the study that produced the primary resource of its period. The final conclusion is that in the Information Age all instruments of national power are now dependent on the macroinvention and its associated resources. This has some similarities with Britain's example in the Age of Steam, whereby one specific instrument of national power became dominant over the others. In the Information Age, the informational instrument is dominant.

The study intentionally cast a wide net in an attempt to garner as many valuable insights as possible. In doing so it introduced multiple complex and interrelated concepts. These included the concepts of macroinventions and microinventions, strategic resources and access, instruments of national power, effects on national security policy, and the concept of techno-resource-dependence transition periods. At times this made the analysis of the examples much more difficult because of the added variables. Future research should instead seek to isolate one or two of these concepts, to explore them more in depth. Below are several questions which may help generate future research topics.

The following questions are in no particular order of importance or precedence. They are offered as potential research topics. Should the U.S. attempt to dissuade allies

---

[178]Committee on Critical Mineral Impacts of the U.S. Economy, 23.

from developing advanced cyber warfare capabilities under the auspice that it will protect them instead? How would such a notion be received? Could there be such a thing as limited cyber warfare? What would it look like and what would be its threshold before invoking all out war? Could there be such a thing as cyber containment? Are there diplomatic negatives to controlling or preventing access to resources in the Information Age? At what point does it become too costly to use economic power? And what is the threshold for applying national military power to prevent or acquire access? Is the U.S. currently in a techno-resource-dependence transition period? If so, is it in the early, middle, or latent stage? And lastly, to what degree can dependence on critical mineral resources in the Information Age be mitigated through alternate means, if any?

This study sought to examine technological strategic resource dependence, its potential for conflict in the twenty-first century, and subsequent influences on U.S. national security policy. The study did not find that technological strategic resource dependence always led to, armed conflict; nor were nations in a constant state of, or preparing for, armed conflict over strategic resources. Instead, the study found that strategic resource dependence more often than not led to economic and informational conflict; with informational conflict increasing as technology progressed. The study's most useful contribution is perhaps the notion of techno-resource-dependence transition periods. It proved very insightful when analyzing the relationships between macroinventions, strategic resources, instruments of national power, and national security policy. Lastly, the study did in fact generate pertinent thoughts concerning resource dependence, the potential for conflict, and subsequent effects on national security policy in the twenty-first century, and in doing so, achieved its intent.

90

BIBLIOGRAPHY

Alperovitz, Gar. *The Decision to Use the Atomic Bomb and the Architecture of an American Myth*. New York: Random House, 1995.

Ashton, Thomas Southcliffe. *Iron and Steel in the Industrial Revolution*. Manchester, ND: Manchester University Press, 1924.

Bacevich, Andrew J. *Long War: A History of U. S. National Security Policy Since World War II*. New York: Columbia University Press, 2009.

Ball, Nicole. *Security and Economy in the Third World*. Princeton, NJ: Princeton University Press, 1988.

Becker, Peter J. "The Role of Synthetic Fuel in World War II Germany: Implications for today?" *Air University Review* (July-August 1981). http://www.airpower. maxwell.af.mil/airchronicles/aureview/1981/jul-aug/becker.htm (accessed 19 September 2012).

Bernstein, Jeremy. *Plutonium: A History of the World's Most Dangerous Element*. Washington, DC: Joseph Henry Press, 2007.

Bose, Meena. *Shaping and Signaling Presidential Policy: The National Security Decision Making of Eisenhower and Kennedy*. College Station, TX: Texas A&M University Press, 1998.

Burgin, Mark. *Theory of Information: Fundamentality, Diversity and Unification*. Hackensack, NJ: World Scientific Publishing Co., 2009.

Cardozier, V. R. *Mobilization of the United States in World War II: How the Government, Military, and Industry Prepared for War*. Jefferson, NC: McFarland and Company, 1995.

Cavelty, Myriam D. *Power and Security in the Information Age*. Abingdon, Oxon: Ashgate Publishing Group, 2008.

Chatterjee, K. K. *Uses of Energy, Minerals and Changing Techniques*. Daryaganj, Delhi, India: New Age International, 2008.

Chollet, Derek. *America Between the Wars: From 11/9 to 9/11: The Misunderstood Years Between the Fall of the Berlin Wall and the Start of the War on Terror*. New York: Public Affairs, 2009.

Church, Roy. *The History of the British Coal Industry, Volume 3 - 1830–1913: Victorian Pre-Eminence*. Oxford: Clarendon Press, 1986.

Churchill, Winston S. *The World Crisis,* Vol. 1. New York: Scribner's, 1923.

Cohen, Benjamin J. *The Question of Imperialism: Political Economy of Dominance and Dependence.* New York: Macmillan, 1974.

Command, Joint Forces. *The Joint Operating Environment (JOE) 2010.* Suffolk, VA: United States Joint Forces Command, 2010.

Committee on Critical Mineral Impacts of the U.S. Economy. *Minerals, Critical Minerals, and the U.S. Economy.* Washington, DC: National Academies Press, 2008.

Coughlin, James R. "What are Cyberspace Operations?" Master's Thesis, Command and General Staff College, Fort Leavenworth, KS, 2012.

Cowley, Robert. *Cold War: A Military History.* Westminster, MD: Random House, 2005.

Crawford, Beverly, and Stafanie Lenway. "Decision Modes and International Regime Change: Western Collaboration on East-West Trade." *World Politics* 37, no. 3 (April 1985): 375-402.

Crump, Thomas. *A Brief History of the Age of Steam: From the First Engine to the Boats and Railways.* London: Avalon Publishing Group, 2007.

Dahl, Erik J. "Naval Innovation: From Coal to Oil." *Joint Forces Quarterly* (Winter 2000-2001): 50-56.

DiNardo, Richard L. *Mechanized Juggernaut or Military Anachronisms? Horses and the German Army of World War II.* Westport, CT: Greenwood Press, 1991.

Doyle, Michael W. *Empires.* Ithica, NY: Cornell University Press, 1986.

Evans, Chris, and Goran Ryden. *The Industrial Revolution in Iron: The Impact of British Coal Technology in Nineteenth-Century Europe.* Burlington, VT: Ashgate Publishing Company, 2005.

Gorski, Richard. *Maritime Labor: Contributions to the History of Work at Sea, 1500-2000.* Amsterdam, Netherlands: Amsterdam University Press, 2008.

Henig, Ruth B. *Origins of the First World War.* Florence, KY: Routledge, 1993.

Hitler's Labor-Front speech in Nuremberg, 12 September 1936.

Huntington, Samuel. "The U.S.-Decline or Renewal?" *Foreign Affairs* 62, no. 2 (Winter 1988/1989): 76-96.

James, Lawrence. *The Rise and Fall of the British Empire.* New York. St. Martin's Press, 1994.

Johnson, Robert. *British Imperialism*. Gordonsville, VA: Palgrave Macmillan, 2003.

Kapstein, Ethan B. *The Political Economy of National Security: A Global Perspective.* New York: McGraw-Hill, 1992.

Karwatka, Dennis. "Thomas Savery and His Steam-Operated Water Pump." *Tech Directions* 66, no. 7 (2007): 100. http://search.proquest.com/docview/ 218494271?accountid=28992 (accessed 25 July 2012).

Kelly, Cynthia C. *Remembering the Manhattan Project: Perspectives on the Making of the Atomic Bomb and Its Legacy*. River Edge, NJ: World Scientific Publishing, 2005.

Kennedy, Paul M. *The Rise and Fall of the Great Powers*. New York: Random House, 1989.

Koistinen, Paul A. C. *Planning War, Pursuing Peace: The Political Economy of American Warfare, 1920-1939.* Lawrence, KS: University Press of Kansas, 1998.

Langer, Howard J. *World War II*. Westport, CT: Greenwood Press, 1999.

Lieber, Keir A. "The Rise of U.S. Nuclear Primacy." *Foreign Affairs* 85, no. 2 (March-April 2006): 42-54.

Lienhard, John H. *How Invention Begins: Echoes of Old Voices in the Rise of New Machines*. Cary, NC: Oxford University Press, 2006.

Martin, Eric, and Sonja Elmquist. "U.S. to File WTO Complaint Over China Rare-Earth Export Caps." 13 March 2012. http://www.bloomberg.com/news/2012-03-13/u-s-will-ask-for-wto-s-help-to-fight-chinese-curbs-on-rare-earth-exports.html (accessed 20 March 2012).

Mason, John W. *The Cold War, 1945-1991*. London: Routledge, 2007.

Massie, Robert K. *Dreadnought: Britain, Germany, and the Coming of the Great War*. New York: Random House, Inc., 1991.

Mendershausen, Horst. *The Economics of War*. New York: Prentice-Hall, 1943.

Mokyr, Joel. *The Lever of Riches: Technological Creativity and Economic Progress*. New York: Oxford University Press, 1990.

More, Charles. *Understanding the Industrial Revolution*. New York: Routledge, 2000.

Murray, Williamson, and Allen R. Millett. *A War to Be Won: Fighting the Second World War, 1937-1945*. Cambridge, MA: Harvard University Press, 2001.

93

————. *Military Innovation in the Interwar Period*. New York: Cambridge University
    Press, 1996.

National Resources Defense Council. "Your Computer's Lifetime Journey."
    http://www.nrdc.org/living/stuff/your-computers-lifetime-journey.asp (accessed
    16 November 2012).

Official Report on German e-crude oil production during World War II.
    http://www.fischer-tropsch.org/primary_documents/gvt_reports/MofFP/
    ger_syn_ind/ (accessed 10 September 2012).

Paret, Peter. *Makers of Modern Strategy: from Machiavelli to the Nuclear Age.* Princeton,
    NJ: Princeton University Press, 1986.

Pomeranz, Kenneth. *The Great Divergence: China, Europe, and the Making of the
    Modern World Economy.* Princeton, NJ: Princeton University Press, 2000.

Redles, David. *Hitler and the Apocalypse Complex: Salvation and the Spiritual Power of
    Nazism.* New York: New York University Press, 2005.

Reinhardt, George C. *Haphazard Years: How America Has Gone to War.* Garden City,
    NY: Doubleday and Company, 1960.

Riley, Jonathon. *Decisive Battles: From Yorktown to Operation Desert Storm.* London:
    Continuum International Publishing, 2010.

Roberts, Paul. *The End of Oil: On the Edge of a Perilous New World.* New York:
    Houghton Mifflin Books, 2004.

Schlesinger, James. *The Political Economy of National Security.* New York: Praeger,
    1960.

Schlager, Neil, and Josh Lauer, ed. "Thomas Newcomen." *Science and Its Times*, Vol. 4.
    Detroit: Gale, 2001. Gale Student Resources In Context, Web, 25 July 2012.

Smil, Vaclav. *Creating the Twentieth Century: Technical Innovations of 1867-1914 and
    Their Lasting Impact.* Cary, NC: Oxford University Press, 2005.

Sokolski, Henry D. "Getting MAD: Nuclear Mutual Assured Destruction, its Origins, and
    Practice." Strategic Studies Institute. November 2004. http://www.strategicstudies
    institute.army.mil/pdffiles/pub585.pdf (accessed 13 August 2012).

Sondhaus, Lawrence. *Naval Warfare, 1815-1914.* New York: Routledge, 2001.

Sutcliffe, Andrea. *Steam: The Untold Story of America's First Great Invention.*
    Gordonsville, VA: Palgrave Macmillan, 2004.

Vagif Agayev, Fuad Akhundov, Fikrat T. Aliyev, and Mikhail Agarunov. "World War II and Azerbaijan." *Azerbaijan International* (Summer 1995): 50-55. http://www.azer.com/aiweb/categories/magazine/32_folder/32_articles/32_ww22. html (accessed 12 September 2012).

Vries, P. H. H. "Are Coal and Colonies really Crucial? Kenneth Pomeranz and the Great Divergence." *Journal of World History* 12, no. 2 (2001): 407-46. http://search.proquest.com/docview/225236235?accountid=28992 (accessed 12 September 2012).

Wells, H. G. *The World Set Free*. London: Macmillan and Company, 1914.

White House. *National Security Strategy*. Washington, DC: Government Printing Office, 2010.

Wilson, Keith. *International Impact of the Boer War*. New York: Palgrave, 2001.

Winton, Harold R. *Challenge of Change: Military Institutions and New Realities, 1918-1941*. Lincoln, NE: University of Nebraska Press, 2000.

Withana, Radhika. *Power, Politics, Law: International Law and State Behavior During International Crises.* Leiden: Martinus Nijhoff Publishers, 2008.

World Nuclear Association. "Online History of Nuclear Energy." Updated June 2010. http://www.world-nuclear.org/info/inf54.html (accessed 28 September 2012).

Yergin, Daniel. *The Prize: The Epic Quest for Oil, Money, and Power.* New York: Simon and Schuster, 1991.

————. *The Quest: Energy, Security, and the Remaking of the Modern World.* New York: The Penguin Press, 2011.

Zelizer, Julian E. *Arsenal of Democracy: The Politics of National Security-From World War II to the War on Terrorism.* New York: Basic Books, 2009.

Zemab, Zbynek A. B. *Uranium Matters: Central European Uranium in International Politics, 1900-1960.* New York: Central European University Press, 2008.

www.ingramcontent.com/pod-product-compliance
Lightning Source LLC
Chambersburg PA
CBHW081841280526
45789CB00007B/2525